CLASSIC WORSHIP
With Brethren in Mind

CLASSIC WORSHIP
With Brethren in Mind

PETER E. ROUSSAKIS

MEETINGHOUSE PRESS
Burlington, Indiana
2005

```
264.06 R762c
Roussakis, Peter E.
Classic worship
```

CLASSIC WORSHIP
With Brethren in Mind

PETER E. ROUSSAKIS

Library of Congress Control Number: 2004109642
International Standard Book Number-13:978-0-9759138-0-8
International Standard Book Number-10:0-9759138-0-8

Copyright 2005 Peter E. Roussakis

All rights reserved. No portion of this material may be reproduced in any way without permission. Unless otherwise noted, all scripture citations are given from the *New International Version*, 1984, International Bible Society.

Printed in the United States of America

Cover Image: *"Washing of the Feet"* by Giotto, c.1304-1306.
Cover/Interior Design: www.book-cover-design.com

MEETINGHOUSE PRESS
P.O. Box 246 • Burlington, IN 46915-0246
765-566-3274 • meetinghousepress@sbcglobal.net

Contents

Preface vii

CHAPTER ONE
Making God Number One 1

CHAPTER TWO
Worshiping the One True God 7

CHAPTER THREE
Keeping the Lord's Day 15

CHAPTER FOUR
Ordering Worship 23

CHAPTER FIVE
Praying in Worship 47

CHAPTER SIX
Praying the Lord's Prayer 59

CHAPTER SEVEN
Preaching with a Manuscript 73

CHAPTER EIGHT
Music in Worship 79

CHAPTER NINE
Rite of Dedication 97

CHAPTER TEN
Signing Repentance 101

CHAPTER ELEVEN
Making a Spiritual Commitment..107

CHAPTER TWELVE
Rites of Christian Baptism & Confirmation 113

CHAPTER THIRTEEN
Church and Membership..121

CHAPTER FOURTEEN
Rite of Holy Communion 137

CHAPTER FIFTEEN
Rite of Feet-washing 147

CHAPTER SIXTEEN
Rite of Anointing..155

CHAPTER SEVENTEEN
The Spiritual Discipline of Fasting 163

Review Guide 169
Index..179
Biography 185

Preface

Planning and conducting services of public worship are the weekly privilege and responsibility of pastors. In some congregations a committee or worship team works with the pastor in the planning process as well as implementation. Needless to say, those serving have the obligation to do everything according to sound biblical principles. Very often, if not most often, evangelical pastors and other worship planners and leaders may have not acquired, due to a lack of study in this area of ministry, an awareness of biblical teaching and the historical expressions of it; that is to say, the time-tested principles and patterns of expression which have grounded Christian corporate worship. Especially in evangelical circles, we pride ourselves on consulting scripture for matters of church life, belief and behavior. Yet somehow it would seem by observation, when it comes to worship matters, many proceed with their ministry as though the scriptures were no longer relevant, a contradiction with regard to what they hold for other matters of their faith and its applications and expressions. However, as with most areas or concerns, when individuals read and study or hear a lecture on a particular topic of interest by someone to whom they are attracted and respect, they become convicted about what is said. In short, they become informed. The present volume is intended to provide the kind of information which will help pastors and parishioners to appreciate what the Bible teaches on matters of public worship, and then hopefully apply them and appropriate applications of them in their own contexts of ministry. In other words, a sound biblical foundation and historical perspective is vital for what we do in worship, how we do it, what is included and in what sensible biblically and theologically-informed order.

CLASSIC WORSHIP

The material presented is called *Classic Worship* because, as with any matter, for example telling time, learning the basics is where one must start, acquiring the fundamentals for a full understanding of the matter. Learning how to tell time with a dial and hands helps persons understand and see why there are sixty seconds in a minute, etc. Then when they read a digital clock, they have a more complete grasp of how we mark and read time.

There are some things which are truly *classics*, whether they are novels, musical works or competitions in the history of sport. We can be inspired by them and learn from them as well. They provide us with excellent models. They are what they are because they have employed the *classical* thinking and are the best expressions of their particular media, skill or form. For example, it would be ridiculous to say to a pole-vaulter or tennis player that no longer do they have to learn their skill or practice their abilities in the ways athletes did in the past, that now there is a more contemporary way to execute their skills. There are simply fundamental ways of understanding and practicing their sports. Similarly, through the years I've taught private piano to many people. And increasingly fewer young people and adults want to learn the skills or understand them. They simply want to play the way they want to play, without the guided instruction or discipline. Needless to say, such persons have never nor will they ever become good pianists to any significant degree. There are some things which are truly classical in their understanding and expression. In the Christian arena, public worship needs no less attention and care.

Many churches have Contemporary services of worship. Some have Blended services, while others retain more Traditional formats. What follows is *not* a critique against utilizing Contemporary or Blended styles. While the term *classic* may be considered a synonym for that which is more traditional, as we think we understand that today, the intention here rather is to communicate that there are truly *classic*, biblical and historical truths, principles and modes of expression of which all involved in planning and leading public worship should be aware, and upon which they may faithfully base and adapt their weekly services of worship. Not to do so would be shirking their responsibility as

Preface

biblically grounded Christians. The congregation which offers a Contemporary service, either as their sole mode of worship expression or in addition to a Blended or Traditional service, would serve itself and its resultant expression well by employing the *classical* principles and inclusions gleaned from Holy Scripture. To do anything less, to throw the baby out with the bathwater, as the saying goes, would demonstrate a lack of biblical attention and integrity. At the close of the chapter on *Ordering Worship* there are examples of both *classic* and contemporary applications of the biblical principles and inclusions presented.

This work is intended for all those interested in and responsible for the preparation and conduct of public worship, and especially for persons within The Brethren Church, headquartered in Ashland, Ohio. In addition, for the benefit of those outside our immediate tradition and those pastors and parishioners new to this community of faith, this volume is offered as a means of introduction to our worship-related distinctives. There are a number of denominations which have the word *Brethren* in their name. They are not all related.

The Brethren Church is one of several denominations with a common heritage dating back to 1708 in Schwarzenau, Germany, where a group of persons convicted that believers' immersion baptism was the biblical pattern of the rite, formed a new fellowship, many of whom emigrated to eastern Pennsylvania in the early 1700's. While there were several designations in existence in the 1800's, the one which became prominent was the German Baptist Brethren, with many congregations in Pennsylvania and Ohio and in other areas south and west. In the 1880's the parent body experienced division into several groups. Several of the denominations which share their roots in the German Baptist Brethren include the Church of the Brethren, The Brethren Church, the Fellowship of Grace Brethren Churches, the Conservative Grace Brethren Church International, the Old German Baptist Brethren, the Old Order German Baptist Church, and the Dunkard Brethren. This writer is affiliated with The Brethren Church, and the contents herein have Brethren in mind. The rites especially are discussed from our particular historic perspective. Dating and gender references are given in the traditional throughout.

CLASSIC WORSHIP

The material is a combination of sermons delivered at the First Brethren Church of Burlington, Indiana, articles and essays. In the first few chapters are offerings which provide a biblical basis and guidance for *Ordering Worship*. The *Ordering* piece is actually a revised address given at the 2003 Indiana District Conference of The Brethren Church held at the Brethren Retreat Center, Shipshewana, Indiana. Two chapters, *Praying in Worship* and *Praying the Lord's Prayer*, offer an overview of the values of congregational prayers and the pastor's leadership.

The above are followed by a brief article on the values of this writer's long-standing preference for *Preaching with a Manuscript,* a piece which several other denominations have requested to be used in their training courses for pastors. An essay on *Music in Worship*, albeit of a more *classic* perspective, gives a theological basis for what may be offered as local church worship music. Both subjects rightly fall within the context of public worship considerations.

The rites and ceremonies as they are understood and practiced in The Brethren Church are given next, interspersed with matters which must logically occur for the rites to be all we believe they should be, represent, and instill. "The ordinances have been the distinctive features of Brethren devotion and worship...[they] are the supreme worship services of the church."[1] Chronologically arranged according to their expected practice, the *Rite of Dedication* of infants is given first. It includes an introduction to the significance of signing faith in general. *Signing Repentance* provides a description of the biblical understandings of repentance as a prelude to why persons need to make peace with God by receiving Jesus Christ as the Savior of their souls and the Lord of their lives. What naturally follows then is a survey of the language used in scripture for *Making a Spiritual Commitment*.

The chapter on the *Rites of Baptism and Confirmation*, which take place after a person makes a commitment to Jesus Christ, gives an explanation of the meanings of Christian believers' baptism and its Brethren administration as three-fold immersion. Because receiving persons into local church membership usually takes place within the

---

[1] Joseph R. Shultz, "Brethren Ordinances," *Report of the Proceedings of the Brethren World Assembly* (Ambler, PA: Brethren Encyclopedia, Inc., 1994), 1. For more on Brethren Worship practices see notes 25, 38, 54, 55, 112, and the Index.

context of a worship service, an essay on the nature of the *Church and Membership* is included next. Within the message on the *Rite of Holy Communion* are related definitions of the terms sacrament, ordinance, and rite, and the practice of the Brethren three-fold administration of feet-washing, a small meal, and the taking of the bread and the cup as the *Love Feast* of the Holy Communion observance. A separate treatment of the *Rite of Feet-washing* is given because of the very special meaning it has, and because its practice in The Brethren Church is unique among Christian traditions today. The *Rite of Anointing* is also one which Brethren Christians especially value and which is offered to those requesting spiritual strength and wholeness during times of particular stress and physical or emotional infirmity.

Although it is not a public worship matter, *fasting* is practiced by many Brethren individuals and congregations. Along with prayer and study it is one of the classic *spiritual disciplines* and may be thought of as a significant means of private worship. A chapter on *The Spiritual Discipline of Fasting* is therefore included.

Pastors should take their responsibility as shepherds seriously for the ministry of worship. Indeed it is most likely the most important ministry in which we are engaged on a weekly basis; thus the primary reason for *Classic Worship: With Brethren in Mind*.

It is the desire of this writer that the material given will assist pastors and parishioners, and especially those in process for ordination or consecration to Brethren ministry, to have a resource on the subject of worship. The collection may be used as reading for study courses in the parish, particularly in Brethren church membership classes. All is offered with the goal that informed worship planners, leaders, and congregations will be more effective and fruitful in their ambassadorship for Jesus Christ.

Expressions of gratitude are extended to my wife, Phyllis, for her patience and support in life and ministry; to my mother, Dorothy, for her life-long encouragement; to the parishioners of the First Brethren Church of Burlington, Indiana, and The Community Church of Alton, New Hampshire for their positive responses and appreciation for classic public worship; and to several persons in academia who have been especially encouraging and influential in shaping my worship and music sensibilities: Hugh T. McElrath and Donald P. Hustad, Southern Baptist Theological Seminary; Horace T. Allen Jr., Boston University; and Arthur J. Dyck, Harvard University.

P. E. R. Spring 2005

CHAPTER ONE

Making God Number One

The Preamble & The First Commandment—Exodus 20:1-3

And God spoke all these words: 'I am the Lord your God, who brought you out of the land of Egypt, out of the land of slavery. You shall have no other gods besides me.'

Every community which exists must have a code of ethics, a set of principles for behavior, or else it won't be a community. The Ten Commandments, the first portion of the ethical instruction given by God to the Israelites, was not only the foundation code which God intended for the Israelites' successful communal organization and behavior, it was the set of principles upon which all the other regulations and ordinances of the covenant were based. Not only so, because Israel was elected by God to be a kingdom of priests to the world, representing God and his ways to the rest of fallen humanity, we learn, therefore, that the Ten Commandments were intended to be the moral standard to be communicated by Israel to all of the other nations of the planet as the code of ethics for humanity.

These *Ten Words*, as they are referred to in the Hebrew, this group of ten statements, also known as the Decalogue, are the most important principles ever revealed to humankind. They represent the supremacy of God; the impossibility of expressing God in any material form; forbidding the reckless use of the name of God; the honoring of parents, thus emphasizing the importance of the family; viewing human life as sacred; demanding sexual purity and fidelity; and preserving the right of human property.[2] In sum, the code demands reverence for God and respect for others.

---

[2]William Barclay, *The Ten Commandments* (Louisville, Kentucky: Westminster John Knox Press, 1998), 2.

Interestingly, the Ten Commandments are actually presented in the same way ancient near eastern treaties were made, including a preamble and then the stipulations; and the language, such as *you shall* and *you shall not*, was the type of usage of such treaties. What we have noted, therefore, is that these ten principles really are a part of a compact, a covenant between God and the Israelites, and by extension of their intention and the Israelites' mission, a covenant with all people.

Preamble

As with the summary of the covenant given in Exodus 19:4-6, the treaty itself begins with a preamble in which God establishes himself as the one who has the authority to present the subsequent covenantal stipulations and obligations. Exodus 20:2 says: "I am the Lord your God, who brought you out of Egypt, out of the land of slavery." It was by God's actions that he is known and which confirms his authority.

The name *Jehovah* (Lord) signifies God's authority, and his right to constrain the Israelites in the ways mentioned in the commands. He reminds them of the recent benefits he has bestowed upon them. The purpose of the first commandment, therefore, is that the Lord wills that he alone be pre-eminent among his people.[3] Further, the words *I am* (v.2) and *You shall have* (v.3) demonstrate the unique *I-Thou* (I-You) relationship between the Creator and his creation, between God and us. We owe our existence to God. He should be number one in our lives. The preamble then is followed by the first word: "You shall have no other gods [besides] me."

First Commandment

Many people--students, college and professional athletes, sports fans--enjoy the hype of being number one. Some take it so seriously, that if they come in second, they stir up trouble. In some instances, such as the World Cup in soccer, people have rioted, looted, and started stampedes which have led to loss of life. Some fans will let nothing get in the way of attending or watching a game. The Bible tells us that the only one who has the right to be number one is God.

---

[3] John T. McNeill, ed. *Calvin: Institutes of the Christian Religion* Vol. 1 (Philadelphia: The Westminster Press, 1960), 382.

The Jews were specifically warned to have no strange gods, no invented gods. God demanded and demands that his people put off "all impiety and superstition, which either diminish or obscure the glory of his divinity."[4] Having a god means accepting and being subject to all the god demands. In forbidding them to worship other gods, God meant they were not to transfer to another what belongs to him, which is our worship, loyalty, love and allegiance.[5]

In Moses' day there were many gods worshiped by the ancient near eastern civilizations. In one sense we could say our God had competition. For example, the Canaanites worshiped Baal, also called Haddad, a storm god (1 Kings 16:31, 18:18-46). They also worshiped Ashtoreth, a mother goddess of fertility (1 Sam. 12:10). The Moabites worshiped Chemosh, their national god of war (Num. 21:29). The Ammonites worshiped Molech (Zeph. 1:5). The Philistines revered Dagon, a grain god (Jud. 16:23). The Sumerians prayed to Tammuz, a storm god (Ezek. 8:14). In Egypt they worshiped Osiris, the god of death, Isis, the goddess of life, and Re, the sun god. In Mesopotamia they worshiped Enlil, the storm god, Ea-Enki, the god of water, Nanna, the moon god, Ishtar, the god of fertility, Ninurta, the war god, and Tiamat, the god of salt water. Jehovah, the one true God of the universe, said we are not to have any other gods in place of him!

There is a story about a hen and a pig. "[One day] a hen and a pig approached a church and read the advertised sermon topic: 'What can we do to help the poor?' Immediately the hen suggested they feed them bacon and eggs. The pig thought for a moment and said: 'There is only one thing wrong with feeding bacon and eggs to the poor. For you it requires only a contribution, but for me it requires total commitment!'"[6] Absolute total commitment to God is impossible in this life, for we are all imperfect. If it were absolutely, totally possible to be absolutely, totally committed to God in all things, there would have been no need for God becoming a person to be the debt payer for our

---

[4]Ibid.

[5]Ibid.

[6]Michael P. Green, ed. *Illustrations for Biblical Preaching* (Grand Rapids: Baker Book House, 1982), 73.

sins. If total spiritual commitment were possible, then we could earn justification. The Bible teaches, however, that "while we were still sinners, Christ died for us" (Rom. 5:8). We have been saved by God's grace, "not of works, so that no one can boast" (Eph. 2:9).

In spite of the fact that it is impossible for anyone of us to be totally and absolutely committed to God in all things, that is exactly what God calls us to be. Through Moses God called: "Hear O Israel. The Lord our God, the Lord is One. Love the Lord your God with all your heart and with all your soul and with all your strength" (Deut. 6:4-5). Jesus, when interrogated by the Pharisees quoted those words as the greatest of God's commandments. Loving the Lord with all your heart and with all your soul and with all your strength is or should be the professed believer's spiritual priority. Seeking God, putting God first above self-interest, making God number one, striving for total commitment of one's being to God, is that to which we are called. Jesus said: "Seek first the kingdom of God" (Mt. 6:33), and then all other things we need will be given.

At this point I want to mention that in Deuteronomy 5 there is the re-stating of the Ten Commandments. As we know, Exodus in the Bible is followed by Leviticus, which presents the regulations for Hebrew worship. Numbers follows, and it reviews the years of wandering, from the time Israel departed from Sinai until, as a new generation, they reached the Jordan River and were about to enter the promised land. Deuteronomy, which means *repetition of the law*, is a book of instructions for the Israelites. It looks backward to what happened to them when they fell away from God. It looks forward with hope, that if God's people would turn from their ways and seek God, worship him alone, and live for him, making God first in their lives, they would be blessed.

Deuteronomy consists of a series of addresses by Moses in his later life. The prominent themes are God's love and the call to total commitment. God's love for his people is declared repeatedly in the book; for example, in chapter 7:7-8 we read: "The Lord did not set his affections on you and choose you because you were more numerous than other peoples. But it was because the Lord loved you and kept the oath he swore to your forefathers that he brought you out with a mighty hand and redeemed you from the land of slavery, from the power of Pharaoh king of Egypt." That love, we must be quick to point out, was also expressed in chastisement. For as faithful and loving parents desire the development of appropriate character and behavior in their children, and sometimes must discipline them to reinforce the understanding of appropriate character and behavior, so also God chooses to discipline his children. The Israelites were delivered, but unfortunately they had to be disciplined, over and over again.

The first four chapters of Deuteronomy are historical in nature. Moses reviewed Israel's history after the Exodus and discussed the lessons which should have been learned. He reviewed their travels, their wandering, and lack of faith, Moses' own failures, and the commissioning of Joshua to lead the Israelites into the Promised Land. In chapter four the call was given to observe and follow the words and ways of the Lord; for if they did, they would be what God wanted them to be, namely ambassadors, his representatives. Of particular importance, of course, was their refraining from engagement in false worship. Speaking for God, Moses said:

> After you have had children and grandchildren and have lived in the land a long time, if you then become corrupt and make any kind of idol, doing evil in the eyes of the Lord your God and provoking him to anger, I call heaven and earth as witnesses against you this day that you will quickly perish from the land that you are crossing the Jordan to possess. You will not live there long but will certainly be destroyed. The Lord will scatter you among the peoples…But if from there you seek the Lord your God, you will find him if you look for him with all your heart and with all your soul (Deut. 4:25-29).

Matthew Henry (1662-1714) commented: "The sin [against the first commandment] which we are most in danger of is giving the glory and honor to any creature which is due to God only. Pride makes a god of self, covetousness makes a god of money, sensuality makes a god of the belly; whatever is esteemed and loved, feared or served, delighted in, or depended on, more than God, that [whatever it is] we do in effect make a god of."[7]

What are some of the other gods which take the place of the one true God in peoples' lives: things, material possessions, money, one's home, even work, a cause, perhaps even one's spouse, a popular figure, another organization, the love of nature, forms of entertainment, one's self? None of these are wrong to care for in and of themselves. We all need and enjoy things. We should all be good stewards of the resources God has given us. We should love our spouses and families, put in a good effort in our work, and have fine, wholesome recreation. However, when any one person, thing or activity usurps the place of number one in our lives, the place reserved for God alone, we are violating the first commandment and insulting God; because in the heart, there's no room for double occupancy. Only one can be number one!

The church is not as strong and productive as it could be most likely because people have divided loyalties. In the words of Joshua I would challenge us: "Choose for yourselves this day whom [or what] you will serve...as for me and my household, we will serve the Lord" (Josh. 24:15). Other than unavoidable work, incapacitation of some form, or extenuating circumstances, professed Christians should be in worship every single Sunday, or else, it would seem, God is not number one.

In a sense, there's no better mirror to see who we really are, where and what our loyalties are, and whose number one than the Ten Commandments. If we gaze in that mirror, we are faced with ourselves. We see our imperfections and our need for a facelift of the heart, surgery of the soul, the need for an antidote for our sinful nature. Galatians tells us that the law was given, among other reasons, to show us our need for God, and to lead us to trust in Christ (Gal. 3:24), the one who offered himself in our place upon the cross of eternity, that by faith in him we might be acquitted of our sin condition and be empowered by his Spirit to strive in love to emulate his character, which is directly reflected in the Ten Words given to the Israelites. Let's make God and his perfect expression, the Lord Jesus Christ, number one in our hearts and living.

---

[7]Matthew Henry, *Matthew Henry's Commentary On the Whole Bible* Vol. 1 (Peabody, Mass: Hendrickson Publishers, 1994), 210.

Chapter Two

Worshiping the One True God

The Second Commandment - Exodus 20:4-6

You shall not make for yourself an idol in the form of anything in heaven above or on the earth beneath or in the waters below. You shall not bow down to them or worship them; for I, the Lord your God, am a jealous God, punishing the children for the sin of the fathers to the third and fourth generation of those who hate me, but showing love to thousands who love me and keep my commandments.

Have you ever heard someone say, or perhaps even you've said, someone is "my idol." When we say that, what we mean is that a particular person is the object of our intense devotion or serves as our highest example. We look to that person as our ideal person, our model. We idolize that person so much that we would like to be just like that person.

Someone might spend so much time doing something, such as working or tending to their *things*, tinkering with a car or whatever, that we could say he or she is obsessed with or idolizes that thing. Still others may latch on to a philosophy of life or some latest mind-set outside of the biblical revelation, and make it their principle for living. Whatever it may be, a person, a thing, a principle or cause, if it is that which holds our highest allegiance, if it takes the place of full recognition of and/or the worship of the one true God, if it is a substitute for full surrender to God as the governing principle of life, we may call it an idol. Idolatry is the worship of that which is other than God. Richard Gorrie has given a fine description of idolatry in the area of other religions.

> In India today it is still quite common for devout Hindus to worship several gods. Some who have been impressed by what they have heard of Christ add the name of Jesus to the list of

their gods. They will tell you that they worship their Hindu gods and *Jesus also*. But when a Hindu becomes a real Christian it is no longer *Jesus also* but *Jesus only* in his life. In [our] country also people have their false gods. Whatever takes the place in [our] thoughts and affections has become a god. The man who gives all his time and thought to making money has made a god of money. The woman who gives all her time and thought to what she wears has made a god of clothing. The person who likes to have a bit of religion in life as just one among many interests is trying to have *Jesus also*. But the true Christian determines to have *no other gods*, whether money, pleasure, sex, sport or anything else. For him it is *Jesus only*. Not that these other things are wrong in their place: but they must take the place of servant not master in our lives.[8]

Here we look to the second commandment of the ten God gave to Moses and the Israelites and other supportive biblical material to help us understand and appreciate foundational principles for worshiping. This may be viewed as the second half of the discussion given previously.

The first commandment is an affirmation of *monotheism*, that there is only one true God. The commandment is given in the form of a prohibition. "You shall have no other gods [besides] me" (Ex. 20:3). It is understood, therefore, that *polytheism*, the worship of more than one god, or the worship of the true God plus other gods, is wrong, because there really is only one true God. Whereas the first commandment focuses on the *object* of our worship, the second commandment addresses an aspect of the manner of our worshiping. "You shall not make for yourself an idol in the form of anything in heaven above or on the earth beneath or in the waters below. You shall not bow down to them or worship them" (Ex. 20:4-5a.). The commandment includes two prohibitions. The first is that God forbids people from making an idol, that is, fashioning a *carved image*, manufacturing or creating a god. We would ask: How could a creature create? How could it be possible for the creat*ed* to fashion a creat*or*? At the very least we would have to

---

[8]Green, 376-377.

say that the nations and tribes of the world who have and continue to do this, have been demonstrating the inner need of all people to want to know and worship their creator. Unfortunately, because they have been going about their search and expression in the wrong manner, they have not come to know who really is the creator. Psalm 96:5 says: "For all of the gods of the nations are idols." Can a carved image communicate? Is that what divinity looks like? Should a god have form? Making a statue of the creator in terms of the created is totally inadequate as a representation of God, for it would be impossible to capture the essence of God's being in terms of anything created.

The Bible says we were created in the image of God, meaning human beings were so created that they have the potentiality to mirror some of the character traits of God. Indeed, that is essential to our reason for existing, making God known through our living. However, God forbids us from trying to image him in the form of anything which exists, the sun, the moon or the stars above, human or animal forms on earth, or the fish in the sea. The ancient Hebrews, and by extension of their commission by God, all of us, are not to make physical representations of God or any other invented gods as objects of worship, because to do so would obscure or mar the true essence and character of the one true God. God says making an idol is wrong, and trying to fashion an image of him is prohibited. That is the first offense. The second is actually bowing down to an idol and worshiping it. What an insult that is to God.

Of course, we know the Israelites did exactly the opposite of God's commandment. Like other ancient peoples around them, they desired to have a *tangible representation* of God. Exodus 32:1-6 records their making the golden calf, or perhaps better rendered the golden bull. In the absence of Moses, who was for them a visible sign and voice for God, they wanted a *visible replacement*. So they made the molten statue and worshiped it. How stupid! They fashioned God in terms of that which was created.

Conversely, how firmly God's commandment became imbedded in the hearts of many Israelites is illustrated by the story of Shadrach, Meshach and Abednego. Because of their refusal "to worship

Nebuchadnezzar's golden image, the king ordered them to be cast into a burning fiery furnace. The Jewish exiles trusted that their God would deliver them, [and] they determined to remain faithful whatever the consequences. [They said:] 'Our God is able to deliver us...But if [he doesn't] be it known unto you, O king, that we will not serve your gods, nor worship the golden image which you have set up'" (Dan. 3:17-18).

To re-emphasize the point, let's ask the question: Why is creating a physical image of God wrong? First, because it adulterates *God's* image. That is, a statue or other manufactured object cannot do justice to the true nature of God. A genuine image of God cannot be found in any one thing or even in a combination of things in the created order.[9] Yes, the Bible says: "The heavens declare the glory of God" (Ps. 19:1), but the heavens are not God. No effort to depict God will be adequate. And no one depiction would satisfy everyone anyway.

Secondly, the prohibition denies that we are the one's who are in charge. Can people evoke the presence of God by any action of their own, by simply fashioning a carved image?[10] Who's in charge anyway? Is it not God who revealed himself through the created order, through his chosen people, through the Holy Scriptures? Which one of us can create out of nothing? Which one of us, apart from the redeeming act of God in Christ, could earn justification for entrance into the kingdom of God's grace? Is it not God who took the initiative to make himself known to us? Creating an image of God is wrong because it obscures the nature of God, which is infinitely-faceted and beyond comprehension. Trying to create an image of God places people on a pedestal not intended for them.

Thirdly, image-making for worshiping is wrong because God is known through the intangible, the spiritual. It is impossible to portray the ineffable in terms of that which is seen and made. A physical representation distorts how and in what way God intended to be revealed, related to and understood. The Bible says that God is insulted when

---

[9] John Calvin, *Calvin's Commentaries* Vol. 2 [Commentaries on the Four Last Books of Moses Vol. 2] (Grand Rapids: Baker Book House, 1993), 108.
[10] H. L. Ellison, *Exodus* (Philadelphia: The Westminster Press, 1982), 107.

his worship is transferred to idols.[11] He is jealous and zealous that he alone be worshiped. God will accept no rivalry or unfaithfulness. He loves us and it matters to him how we think of him.[12]

Interestingly enough, there have been in recent years attempts to re-image God, as if that were conceivable. For example, at a conference in Minneapolis in the 1990's female participants fashioned what looked like a papier-mâché idol and worshiped it as though it were the goddess Sophia.[13]

In the second commandment God was saying to the Hebrews that idols are entanglements. Idols for God or of false gods cause people to miss the point of how God is to be known, related to, and worshiped. True worship is a matter of inner faith; it takes place in the heart, as Jesus explained in his conversation with the Samaritan woman. Our Lord said: "The true worshipers will worship the Father in spirit and in truth. God is spirit, and his worship must be worship in spirit and in truth" (from Jn. 4:23-24). What did Jesus mean by *in spirit and in truth*?

The Israelite tradition of worship was based on the observance of externals including ceremonies and sacrifices. Some may have viewed acceptable devotion as merely keeping the regulations, observing the feasts, or going to a sacred location such as Jerusalem, even if their hearts were not genuinely, spiritually right with God. Jesus made the point that the manner of true worship of the one true God emanates from the heart, from the inner self, the person's spirit. True worshipers worship God with their hearts. That's what is meant by *in spirit*.

---

[11] *Calvin's Commentaries* Vol. 2 [Commentaries on the Four Last Books of Moses, Vol. 2], 109.

[12] Ellison, 107.

[13] Susan Cyre, "Fallout Escalates Over Goddess Sophia Worship," *Christianity Today* (Vol. 38, No. 4, April 4, 1994), 74. A significant summary of some of the trends of other current idolatrous theology is given in Frederic B. Burnham, ed. *Postmodern Theology* (New York: Harper & Row, 1989), 66-71. Other volumes which explore re-imaging God include Sallie McFague, *Models of God* (Philadelphia: Fortress Press, 1987), and Sallie McFague's *Metaphorical Theology: Models of God in Religious Language*. Fortress Press, 1982. A good response to criticisms made of the use of masculine language for God in the Bible is given by Elizabeth Achtemeier in "Why God is not Mother," *Christianity Today* (Vol. 37, No. 9, August 16, 1993).

The plain meaning of *in truth* is *genuinely*. The word in the original conveys the idea of realness or genuineness. True worship happens when people worship not with man-made objects, but with their inner selves being genuinely responsive to the love of God, and genuinely open to the will of God. The essence of true worship is not so much *outer* observance as it is an *inner*, genuine, spiritual response. Without the inward movement of the heart, all outer observances are meaningless in God's view. Why is this so? Because God is known through spiritual discernment. *Knowledge* of God is not acquired through outward means, but by *inward faith*. We may become *aware* of the existence of God through externals (e.g. nature, stained-glass windows, etc.), but knowledge of God, *knowing* God is possible only through the spoken word, and the inward faith response to it. Ceremonies, architecture, other physical aids and gestures and sounds are all fine and meaningful ways of signing and symbolizing spiritual realities. They can be helps in directing our minds, so long as they do not obscure the plain truth of God who revealed and who reveals himself inwardly. A carved image or any other thing in creation cannot provide knowledge or establish a relationship. A carved image is not personal. It has no feelings and it cannot relate.

From these understandings of the second commandment and Jesus' conversation with the Samaritan woman, what conclusions may we draw? To review, the second commandment forbids the use of the making of statues or pictures of God as objects of worship. Made-up portraits of Jesus as *aids* to devotion, it seems to me, should be used sparingly. No manufactured idols as representative of the triune God are possible or appropriate. Jeremiah said idols are like scarecrows in a melon patch. They cannot speak and they have no life-giving strength (10:5). Christian symbols such as crosses, bread, the cup, baptismal water, basins and towels are all useful aids to devotion. However, most Protestant church sanctuaries are fairly unornamented so as to focus attention on the spoken and sung words of God which appeal more to our inner selves, where the true seat of devotion lies.[14]

---

[14]This matter was discussed by both John Wesley, *The Works of John Wesley*, third edition, Vol. X (Grand Rapids: Baker Book House, 1991), 109; and by John Calvin, *Calvin's Commentaries* Vol. 2 [Commentaries on the Four Last Books of Moses, Vol. 2], 108.

Secondly, whereas God gave Moses the Ten Words of covenant and morality, so he has made his complete revelation known to us through the writings of Holy Scripture. It is God's word to which we are drawn to understand who he is and how we are to worship him. Scripture says God is primarily spirit and he seeks the adoration of our spirits. So we must stick to the scriptures. To do otherwise is to err.

A third principle we may discern is that Jesus Christ is the only legitimate image of God we are given. The apostle Paul wrote to the Colossian church: "He is the image of the invisible God..." (Col. 1:15; see also 2 Cor. 4:4). We are to focus on him as our conception of God, for he was God incarnate, the Word become flesh. 1 John 2:23 says: "Whoever has not the Son has not the Father." When we know Christ, we know God.

Fourth, God is known through spiritual discernment. God and God's truths have been revealed to us in our inner being through the Spirit.

> ..."No eye has seen, nor ear has heard, no mind has conceived what God has prepared for those who love him" —but God has revealed it to us by his Spirit. The Spirit searches all things, even the deep things of God. For who among men knows the thoughts of a man except the man's spirit within him? In the same way no one knows the thoughts of God except the Spirit of God. We have not received the spirit of the world but the Spirit who is from God, that we may understand what God has freely given us. This is what we speak, not in words taught us by human wisdom but in words taught by the Spirit, expressing spiritual truths in spiritual words. The man without the Spirit does not accept the things that come from the Spirit of God, for they are foolishness to him, and he cannot understand them, because they are spiritually discerned. (1 Cor. 2:9-14)

A fifth conclusion is drawn directly from the commandment. Those who transgress God's law by manufacturing idols of God or creating false gods of things, people or misguided thought forms, will incur the consequences expressed; "...for I, the Lord your God, am a jealous God, punishing the children of the fathers to the third and fourth generation of those who hate me." We understand this statement in the context of the Israelite home. That is, the extended family, usually upwards possibly to the fourth generation, lived together. Therefore, if one, particularly the spiritual head of the family, goes astray, setting a pattern of false worship or no worship at all, the rest of the family will be affected and probably will go astray as well. Hence, the importance of *spiritually-correct* parents. Idolatry is an affront to God's majesty, a violation of his covenant, and the ruin of families. On the other hand, as verse six of Exodus 20 says, God will extend his favor to a thousand generations, that is, the effect of faithfulness will last a long time and be carried through from generation to generation to generation when families worship as God intended.

Sixth, attempting to alter or re-invent God is a form of idolatry. It is wrong. John Calvin (1509-1564) said that when people use their imaginations and try to create God according to their own reason, God's worship has been profaned, and in a way they metamorphose him.[15] Bible expositor Matthew Henry put it this way: "Our religious worship must be governed by the power of faith, not by the power of imagination."[16] Certainly our worship is enhanced by the imaginative, the creative, the artistic. However, it should be ruled and directed by faith in Christ and the revealed written word of God. We know God primarily by faith (Gal. 3:25-4:7), by faith in Jesus who was *the* one and only image of the invisible God.

Finally, if there is any one, any thing, or any philosophy of life which is usurping the place of God as the center of our lives, that is an idol; and, as Paul said to the Thessalonians, we are to "turn to God from idols to serve the living and true God" (1 Th. 1:4; see also Gal. 4:8-10). Making God number one in our lives and worshiping the one true God are priority messages of the scriptures. Let's permit these commandments to have full sway in our lives, to help us continue to so live and worship that God will increasingly be glorified in our hearts, in our living, our relating, and in all our activities.

---

[15] *Calvin' Commentaries* Vol. 2, 107, and Vol. XVII Commentary on the Gospel According to John. Vol. 1, 160.

[16] Matthew Henry, 210.

Chapter Three
Keeping the Lord's Day

The Fourth Commandment - Exodus 20:8-11

Remember the Sabbath day by keeping it holy.
Six days you shall labor and do all your work, but the seventh day
is a Sabbath to the Lord your God. On it you shall not do any work,
neither you, nor your son or daughter, nor your manservant or
maidservant, nor your animals, nor the alien within your gates.
For in six days the Lord made the heavens and the earth, the sea, and
all that is in them, but he rested on the seventh day. Therefore the
Lord blessed the Sabbath day and made it holy.

We are going to focus on the first part of the commandment: "Remember the Sabbath day by keeping it holy. Six days you shall labor and do all your work, but the seventh day is a Sabbath to the Lord your God. On it you shall not do any work..." In the course of our interpretation we will need to define Sabbath, holy, and work; and then we'll trace the development of how and why Christians have come to worship on the first day of the week.

Interpretation

The Israelites in Egypt were accustomed to a ten day week. They may not have had a day of rest. So when God set out to assist his chosen people to become orderly, healthy, worshipful and righteous, he gave them commandments, regulations and ordinances which would facilitate their development and which would be God-honoring. One of those helps was the establishment of how many days to work, and when to rest and worship. In the *fourth commandment what is presented is the sanctification of time.* All time is of God. To work all of the time for one's own gain, however, would be totally self-serving, it would be physically exhausting, and also would make it impossible to do those things which creatures should do to honor their creator, the one who created them and blessed them with time. So God instituted the seven day week, something with which the Israelites were also familiar, for the Babylonians observed a seven day week, most likely regulated by the pattern of the moon. God likened their weekly cycle to the account of creation, an account which, it seems to me, was inspired not so much to describe God's exact pattern of creation, as it was to give the Israelites a big hint, that they should work for six days, then take a day for rest and for specifically God-honoring thinking and worshiping.

The Hebrew word *shabbat*, from which the term Sabbath is derived, means to cease, to desist, to rest from laboring. On that seventh day of the week for the Israelites, they were not to be engaged in the work they did normally on the other six. The seventh day for them was to be a Sabbath, a rest and worship day. In other words, that day was to be kept holy, a God-honoring day, separated from the other days of the week as uniquely, distinctly a day for remembering upon whom we depend for all things. *The Sabbath day, the rest and worship day, was considered to be a sign of the Covenant made between God and the Israelites, just as the rainbow was the sign of God's covenant with Noah* (see Ex. 31:12-18 & Ezek. 20:12, 20 as a sign of the covenant).

So *Sabbath* means rest. *Holy* means, separate, different, devoted to God; and the work they were not to do was the work they did on the other six days, that is, their *occupational work*. That the Sabbath included worship as well as rest is attested to by Psalm 92, called a psalm for the Sabbath day. "It is good to praise the Lord and make music to your name, O most High, to proclaim your love in the morning and your faithfulness at night..." (vv. 1-2).

By the time of Jesus, excessive added regulations had been made by rabbis regarding what the Jews could or could not do on the Sabbath. Such Jewish legalism included it being forbidden to tie a knot, to light a fire, to move a lamp, or to prepare a meal.[17] Instead of it being a day designed to protect the rights and the health and welfare of workers and families, as well as to worship God, the Sabbath increasingly became a day of prohibitions,[18] something Jesus would challenge during his ministry.

---

[17] Barclay, *The Ten Commandments*, 18.
[18] Ibid., 18-19.

Many have asked, if the Ten Commandments are a binding moral code, and the fourth commandment specifies the keeping of the seventh day, why do most Christians not observe it? What led to the development of the Christian observance of worship on the first day of the week? We will discern several stages in the development.

Exploration

As we explore the answers to these questions, we will do ourselves a favor by understanding from scripture a couple of principles of biblical revelation. First, not all ceremonies of regulations given to the Israelites are binding for all peoples, as we shall see from the teaching of the apostle Paul. The ceremonial regulations for Jews in former days are not necessarily binding for Gentiles, although certain principles remain. Secondly, as illustrated by the scriptural revelation regarding the afterlife, specifically *sheol, hades and hell*, there are subjects which have a developed revelation, based most likely on the readiness God saw the people had for comprehending such things. And, of course, in the case of *sheol, hades and hell*, the fullness of understanding could not have been revealed until the Messiah had come, and belief or non-belief in him became the new testament, the new pattern of accountability.

Such is the case regarding Sabbath observance, because Christians in the days of the growing church began meeting on the first day of the week, commemorating the resurrection of Jesus. As the early church developed, there were Jewish Christians, then Gentile converts, and in many congregations there was a mixture. Along with that mixture were differing opinions and attitudes regarding rest and worship. Many Jewish Christians observed the Sabbath, the seventh day, and met with their fellow Christians on the first day of the week. Gentile Christians did not have the Sabbath tradition to which to relate, so they simply met on the first day of the week to remember Jesus. Acts 20:7 says: "On the first day of the week we came together to break bread. Paul spoke to the people." The expression *break bread* did not refer simply to having a meal, but rather this phrase was an abbreviated way of saying they shared the bread and the cup of Holy Communion instituted by Jesus as a tangible aid to remembering him. Also, from other historical accounts, it seems that early on Christians did have a meal of which the bread and the cup of Holy Communion were integral ingredients. So in the developing church, Christian worship was held on the first day of the week. It included the *remembrance of Jesus' death and resurrection in Holy Communion, and it included speaking.*

1 Corinthians 16:2 is another reference to the first day of the week. In this verse Paul says that the meeting day should also be one where the faithful think of the needs of others. "On the first day of every week, each one of you should set aside a sum of money in keeping with his income, saving it up, so that when I come no collections will have to be made." Here we learn that they met every week on the first day, and that the meeting included *receiving offerings.*

At this point, as far as the Gentile Christians were concerned, we have no mention of their doing or not doing any work on their worship day. For the Jewish Christians, matters regarding the use of the worship day may have begun to loosen up a bit because of Jesus' previous teaching. For example, when questioned by the Pharisees regarding his healing on the Sabbath, as recorded in Mark 2:27, Jesus replied: "The Sabbath was made for man, not man for the Sabbath." What he meant was that the Sabbath was given to them originally to benefit them, for them to be refreshed from their labor. People were not created to benefit a Sabbath. Yes, they were honoring God by observing the Sabbath day as holy. However, Jesus challenged the Pharisaic, legalistic interpretation of observing the Sabbath, as he challenged them on their interpretation of other commandments, such as murder and adultery (e.g. Mt. 5:21-22, 27-28). So in Jesus' teaching we have the rejection of the Pharisaic regulations and interpretations, and the matter of the use of the rest and worship day, which may include the care of the needs of others (see also Mt. 5:17-20 & Mk. 7:9-13).

Another element in the development of the Christian rest and worship day was Paul's teaching of the *new covenant.* For example, in 1 Corinthians 11:26 Paul cites Jesus' words regarding Holy Communion: "This cup [represents] the new covenant in my blood; do this, whenever you drink it, in remembrance of me." Remembering Jesus, who came to offer a new covenant, a new testament, a new pattern for any and all peoples being in right relationship with God, through his sacrifice and through our commitment to him, superceded, took the place of and nullified the older covenantal pattern (not the principle, but the pattern). Paul was inspired of God to realize that in Christ God was now "fulfilling a new and cosmic purpose."[19] The law would take a secondary place. It was then Jesus, and not the law or the Mosaic covenant that had become the centerpiece of God's saving work for both Jews and Gentiles.[20]

Moreover, regarding the Christian rest and worship day, emerging seemed to be a recognition that built into the fabric of human life was an awareness of the need for a day of rest and worship at regular intervals, as attested to in the Genesis creation account and in the fourth commandment. However, what was now *the supreme reason* for meeting and worshiping and caring for others was more importantly the death and resurrection of Jesus, who made all things new, the new spiritual creation of life in those who surrender their hearts to him as the Savior of their souls and the Lord of their lives; Jesus, who met with us, cared for us, paid our debt of sin, and who promises us that same resurrection.

And so Paul, formerly a Pharisee and devoted Jew, viewed any attempt to impose Sabbath keeping, that is the seventh day rest and worship day, upon Gentile Christians as wrong. Romans 14:5-6 says: "One man considers one day more sacred than another; another man considers every day alike. Each one should be fully convinced in his own mind. He who regards one day as special, does so to the Lord..." (see also Gal. 4:8-11). Paul allowed for the keeping of such special days as the Jewish Sabbath as a matter of individual conscience. This is an example of developed revelation.

Stages of Development

What we have learned, given all of the above, are several stages in the development of the Christian rest and worship day. *Stage one* is that

---

[19]D.A. Carson, ed. *From Sabbath to Lord's Day: A Biblical, Historical and Theological Investigation* (Grand Rapids: Academie Books, 1982), 161.
[20]Ibid.

which came from the *Old Testament revelation*. Awareness and respect for the seven day pattern of living which God instituted. Six days a week may be devoted to occupational work. One day a week should be set aside for worship and physical and spiritual refreshment, refraining from one's occupational work.

Stage two may be identified as that which is discerned from *the teaching of Jesus*. Our Lord's interpretation of the law taught that cessation of all activity on the rest and worship day was not the original intent and may include, for example, acts of kindness for others.

Stage three includes *early Christian practice and instruction as given in Paul's letters*. This reveals that the emerging Christian worship and rest day was on the first day of each week, and included speaking, singing (e.g. Col. 3:16), and collecting for the needs of others (see also 1 Cor. 14:26-40).

By the end of the New Testament we have the *fourth and last biblical stage revealed*, the use of *the term for the Christian rest and worship day* which would become the traditional language for centuries to come. In Revelation 1:10 we read John saying: "On the Lord's Day I was in the Spirit..." Considering the fact that the Revelation of John was written around 100 A.D., we have the indication that some thirty or more years from Paul's writings, the practice of the Christian worship day and the terminology referring to it were fairly well established. It was the *Lord's Day*. The reason we may make this judgment is the fact that so many other writers from the time of John's revelation onward referred to Sunday as the Lord's Day, the day upon which Christian worship was held. The worship orders which are known to us from this time onward all attest to Christians gathering on the first day of each week, called the Lord's Day, for praying, the reading and interpretation of God's written word, singing, partaking of the bread and the cup, and collecting for the needs of the saints, every time they met.

We need to be reminded: "Christian Sunday worship did not originate as a replacement for the Jewish Sabbath, but as the new, specifically Christian day of worship..."[21] Of course attempts were made, even during the ancient church period, to legally regulate what some called

---

[21] Ibid., 273.

the Christian Sabbath. However, in the fourth century, on March 3, 321, a most significant event took place. Emperor Constantine made a law requiring total, public rest from occupational work on Sunday. Sunday became a legal, holy day. And through the years there have been further attempts by various Christian traditions and social groups to apply regulations for the day, just as the Rabbis and Pharisees had done for the Sabbath. In our own country *blue laws* were made for that purpose.

So whereas Jesus came not to do away with the law, but to fulfill it, to help us understand its intent for the well-being of all, so also the observance intended in the fourth commandment, in light of the new covenant, is the observance of one day in seven as *a* Sabbath, a day of worship and rest from occupational work, for strengthening the moral fiber of life, a day to honor God, a day specifically to remember and pay tribute to Jesus. The Lord's Day may include any activity which honors God and furthers his work. It may be a day for study of his word, a day for prayer and fellowship, worship, enjoying family and friends. Employing the teachings of Jesus and Paul, however, we must leave any further specific uses of the day as a matter of individual conscience. And we must respect one another's views, not pass judgment, and not regulate.

CHAPTER FOUR
Ordering Worship

John R. W. Stott, one of the finest preachers and Bible expositors of the second half of the twentieth century, and Pastor Emeritus of All Souls Church in London, has been a favored speaker in our country in evangelical circles. Under his preaching in 1969 at Urbana, Illinois, I was convicted to offer my life for full-time Christian service as God might lead. John Stott has written many books, not the least of which is his masterful commentary on Romans.[22] Whenever I hear of a book or other resource from his pen or voice I make a point of availing myself of his wisdom and insight. Having been a musician for many years with a keen interest in worship, I am especially watchful of materials in those areas. To my great joy, some time ago, I read of a tape recording available of John Stott speaking to a convention in Atlanta on the subject of worship.[23] Nothing for me could have been more exciting: John Stott and worship. I secured the tape and listened intently. Stott said one should never have to choose between worship and witness. Both are necessary and important aspects of what it means to be a faithful Christian in ministry. We worship, in part, that we may be inspired to witness. We witness that others will be moved to give their lives to God and worship him aright. Worship and witness go hand in hand. However, as John Stott commented, if he had to choose which one, worship or witness, was/is the priority task of the Christian community, he would have to choose worship, for all our worshiping and working for the Lord is ultimately done so that God will receive the honor due his holy name, that as many people as possible will come to faith and commitment and put him first in their lives. Besides, in the heavenly realm we shall be worshiping God for ever and ever!

Worshiping with the community of faith is what God expects. "Come, let us worship and bow down; let us kneel before the Lord our

---

[22]John R. W. Stott, *Romans* (Downers Grove, Illinois: InterVarsity Press, 1994).

[23]John R. W. Stott, "Reality in Worship" (Chattanooga, Tennessee: The Tape Ministry, @1972, exact date unknown).

maker. For he is our God, and we are the people of his pasture, and the sheep of his hand" (Psalm 95:6-7 KJV). "On the first day of the week we came together to break bread. Paul spoke to the people...until midnight" (Acts 20:7). Worshiping is the priority task of ministry. It is the main event, if you will, when the family of faith gathers each week. We gather to offer praise to God; to confess sins and acknowledge our dependence upon God; to hear the Bible read, proclaimed and related to our lives; and to be inspired and challenged to live as our Lord, the prophets and the apostles taught. Yet how do pastors know what to do in worship? What do the scriptures teach regarding the inclusions of public services of worship, and in what order the elements should be arranged?

We shall consider an overall two-fold purpose of worship, its characteristics, order and inclusions, and a word about the two main historic influences which helped shape early Christian worship.

Purposes of Worship

There are many reasons why we come together for worship. The various elements of the order of service indicate some of them. However, the overall purposes of group worship are two. First, we come together to honor God, to extol the triune God who is our Creator, without whom we would not exist, without whom we would not be cared for, provided for and sustained. David rightly admonished the Israelites, as given in Psalm 29:1-2: "Ascribe to the Lord, O mighty ones, ascribe to the Lord glory and strength. Ascribe to the Lord the glory due his name; worship the Lord in the splendor of his holiness." We come together to glorify God, to praise his name, to thank him, to declare the worth-ship of God.

The second purpose of corporate worship is given in Paul's teaching. We gather that we may encourage one another and be built up in faith. 1 Corinthians 14:26 says: "When you come together, everyone has a hymn, or a word of instruction, a revelation, a tongue or an interpretation. All of these must be done for the strengthening of the church." We come to worship to give glory to God. We come as well to edify the Body of Christ. We come to salute God! We also come to be strengthened in the faith and to help strengthen our fellow believers. The glorifying of God and the building up of the family of faith are the two overall purposes of our worshiping.

Biblical Worship

In evangelical circles there have been many discussions and books written over the past thirty years regarding worship. In a way, they are catching up with the mainline churches which have been doing so since fifty years earlier. Changes in styles of music and ways of enacting various elements abound. Unfortunately, however, we are aware that many churches have found their congregations polarized, and some have been fractured because of the ways newer forms of expression have been introduced or forced upon them. Discussions continue.

However, the one area of conversation which seems to be lacking significantly in these discussions and writings, an aspect of worship which may be one of the keys to providing more healthful and congenial attitudes and thinking about it is that of *worship order*. Some people probably think that they would be stepping on other peoples' toes, or that others might view in any discussion of worship order a lack of respect for the various traditions which exist. To be sure, respect and appreciation are appropriate. However, in free-church traditions such as ours, where there is no denominationally prescribed *liturgy*, that is, no suggested set order for public services of worship, there has been, at least by my observation of free-church worship orders over the past thirty years of my active ministry, very little understanding or even interest on the part of the clergy in this area. Consequently, from one church to the next there seems to be no rhyme or reason displayed by many worship orders. It would seem pastors have not really included in their list of commitments, doing their homework on what the Bible and the early church have said and practiced. To be sure, the church of the New Testament was emerging and developing. Christians through the centuries have and continue to study the scriptures for guidance and principles for the shaping of decisions and policies in many areas, such as ordination, baptismal and Holy Communion practices. How did the early Christians, the elders and parishioners go about their worshiping?

What did they understand as biblical teaching, that which may be appropriate biblically speaking? What were the influences which shaped known early Christian worship orders?

In the tape recording mentioned above John Stott cited three characteristics of worship worthy of note, characteristics worship planners should keep in mind when they prepare for their weekly services. Stott said the first characteristic is that worship should be informed and inspired by the Holy Scriptures. Worship should be *biblical.* That is, worship service orders and inclusions should be biblically informed, grounded and arranged. The elements and their order should be based upon biblical understanding, suggestion and example. In other words, whatever we do in and through the church, we should be going by the *Book*, doing things *God's way.*

You may remember the story in Leviticus 9 and 10 regarding Aaron and his sons beginning their priestly duties. They were to follow God's instructions regarding the consecration of themselves and the furnishings connected with worship. George Knight gives an account of what transpired.

> We learned in chapter 8 that the holy fire was kept going continually on the altar and that it alone was to be used for the sacrificial processes that maintained Israel's fellowship with God. For it had come down from God and had not been kindled by the hand of man (9:24). This holy fire alone was to be used, "taken from off the altar." Then again, no unsanctified person had the right merely to march into the sanctuary without going through the necessary ritual process before handling the holy things that marked the presence of the holy God. What these two men--sons of Aaron!--did was this. On a pan filled with hot ashes from an unconsecrated fire taken from somewhere else outside the "holy" precincts, they laid incense which was to go up into God's nostrils as an acted prayer. (The composition of this expensive incense, by the way, is described at Ex. 30:34-38.) This action of theirs was, of course, no mere peccadillo. It was a flagrant piece of disobedience and disloyal-

ty to God. These men were virtually saying, "Our fire is as good as yours, God. We don't need yours."...Their action came under the category of "sins with a high hand," and so was worthy of death.[24]

Aaron's sons did not do things God's way; for us, the way the Bible instructs, either by specific command or by principle. The consequence of a poor worship order may not be death to the pastor, although parishioners may sense things could be otherwise, and a poor worshiping experience may lead to dissatisfaction with the pastoral leadership. It may not be the death of the congregation, although substance-less services will leave parishioners unfed and eventually starving or apathetic. The point is that we should go about planning and conducting worship God's way. What does the Bible say regarding worship order?

Order of Worship

In 1 Corinthians we read Paul's exhortations to the Christians in Corinth. Their worshiping, particularly their observance of the Lord's Supper, was disorderly. He wrote: "When you come together... [everything] must be done for the strengthening of the church." Verse thirty-three says: "...God is not a God of disorder but of peace." In verse forty he said: "...everything should be done in a fitting and orderly way." Paul advocated orderliness about the affairs of the house of the Lord (1 Tim. 3:15). The skeletal order for worship has for centuries been commonly accepted and derived from the classic passage often cited in Isaiah 6, the vision of Isaiah through which the prophet, ministering in Judah, the southern of the two kingdoms of the Israel and Judah, received his call. He experienced this vision @736 B.C., the year Uzziah, King of Judah, died. Isaiah 6:1-4 says:

> In the year that King Uzziah died, I saw the Lord seated on a throne, high and exalted, and the train of his robe filled the temple. Above him were seraphs, each with six wings: With two wings they covered their faces, with two they covered their feet, and with two they were flying. And they were calling to

---

[24]George A. F. Knight, *Leviticus* (Philadelphia: The Westminster Press, 1981), 58.

one another: "Holy, holy, holy is the Lord Almighty; the whole earth is full of his glory." At the sound of their voices the doorposts and thresholds shook and the temple was filled with smoke.

We discern the first ingredient in what may be viewed as a skeletal outline for public worship to be *adoration*. The first thing we should be doing in worship is praising God. Most congregations are aware of that and usually do so in their services.

Next we look to verses five through seven.

"Woe to me!" I cried. "I am ruined! For I am a man of unclean lips, and I live among a people of unclean lips, and my eyes have seen the King, the Lord Almighty." Then one of the seraphs flew to me with a live coal in his hand, which he had taken with tongs from the altar. With it he touched my mouth and said, "See, this has touched your lips; your guilt is taken away and your sin atoned for."

In his visionary state Isaiah realized his unworthiness and unrighteousness before a holy God. He *confessed* his sinfulness, which is followed by a declaration of *pardon*. Perhaps a case could be made here, although not a strong one, for *proclamation* in both verses three and seven. Adoration is followed by confession and pardon. Do your worship orders include an act of confession by the people?

The Isaiah outline for worship then concludes with an invitation to commitment, followed by the offering of self. Verse eight reads:

Then I heard the voice of the Lord saying, "Whom shall I send? And who will go for us?" And I said, "Here am I. Send me!"

Do your worship orders include the elements of response as the last section of the service? That is, do you sing a hymn or offer an affirmation of faith, take the offering and extend an invitation to commitment following the spoken word?

From the Old Testament, therefore, one of the passages which provides guidance in developing a worship order is Isaiah 6 where are suggested *adoration*, followed by *confession*, an expression of *pardon* and an act of *dedication*. As given here and for example in Genesis 1, the scripture reveals our God is a God of order. One implication is that we should be biblically intelligent and orderly in our worship planning and conduct. In The Brethren Church the pattern derived from the Isaiah 6 passage "has received widespread use," with suggested worship service orders published in years past.[25]

I will never forget my beginning days of ministry in Burlington in the fall of 2000. Honestly and sincerely, I inherited an extremely unbiblically informed order of worship. It was one of the worst I'd ever seen. I will refrain from a thorough analysis of it here, although I am prepared to give one. I told my wife that I thought it would be best to make any changes at a slow pace, to teach about worship from the pulpit, and to add or amend elements gradually. I adjusted the order with which they had been accustomed in modest fashion and we conducted our first service with the Burlington Brethren. Afterwards, my wife, Phyllis, said to me: "Are you really going to go that slow?" So during the next week I gave the matter much thought and prayed daily for guidance in the matter. I came to the conclusion that since the congregation was very biblically concerned and astute, that I would preach on the subject and introduce an order which reflected the scriptural grounding given above. The immediate response was not what I anticipated. I thought people might be cautious or questioning, perhaps even silent. They were not. At the receiving line after the service, many persons had tears in their eyes. Some could not even speak because they were so overcome with emotion. The comment of one tearful woman expressed the sentiment of most as it turned out: "Thank you, it has been so long since we've worshiped."

Many of their practices remain. Musically we still have choruses as well as hymns. We still have song leaders. There is "special music" of

---

[25]Kenneth I. Morse. "Worship, Public," *The Brethren Encyclopedia* Volume Two, Donald F. Durnbaugh, editor (Philadelphia, PA and Oak Brook, IL: The Brethren Encyclopedia, Inc., 1983), 1377. The complete article, pp. 1373-1379 is an historical digest of the public worship practices of the Brethren up to the time of publication. At the close is a substantial bibliography of source readings.

whatever style of interest to the musician. And yes, we still sing "Happy Birthday" to those being remembered during the Church Concerns before the actual beginning of worship (something into which I had to grow). We still have a parishioner read scripture. What made the difference? Yes, it was in part the order. As we will discuss later, it was also because the congregation was involved more than merely singing. It was *their* order, *their* worship. The service had a substantially biblically informed shape. And even though parishioners were unable to articulate their thoughts and feelings, it was clear they were moved. The order itself took on a sacred significance beyond which words can describe, like the special meaning the praying of the Lord's Prayer or the reciting of Psalm 23 might have for people, especially at memorial services. The order and the congregational participation made the difference.

There was a time in American free-church tradition congregations when there was more attention paid to the order of worship. Then in the 1800's because of the influence and pattern of Camp Meeting Revival services, many churches supplanted their traditional orders with that of the revivals with their longer times of singing, which in those days was with a plethora of gospel songs, and with the sermon as the second half of the service. In the last century with the influence of the Charismatic Movement, particularly in the 1970's onward, and the resultant emergence of contemporary Christian music, another pattern of worshiping publicly emerged. Based on these historical movements and their effects on worshiping, I believe the question may be asked: *should the music of worship dictate and drive the course of public worship, which seems to have been and is the case for many; or should worship be informed and shaped by biblical understanding and principle?* I am a musician, and I value greatly the ministry music plays in worship and church life in general. Far be it from me to devalue music. I have served as a minister of music and taught church music and worship at both the undergraduate and graduate levels. I'm very thankful God gave me interests, a measure of native proclivity and ability, as well as formal training. Far be it from me, however, to permit the music to be the basis upon which we design and conduct worship. The *Book* should do that. God's principles, the revelation of such matters in scripture, should be our source of information and guidance in ordering worship. Worship should be *biblical*.

What is your church's worship order like? Do you know why you do what you do? Do you think the order of service is sufficiently biblically informed? Pastors, do your orders of service demonstrate and teach what are God's principles for public worship? Do you have an act of confession in your service (an element which seems to be lacking in many evangelical worship services)? Oh, some may say, such "formal" orders do not relate to people today. Oh really? Let me quote from a recent UPI article. Dr. Uwe Siemon-Netto, Religion Correspondent for UPI reported:

> A new generation of worshipers is confounding pastors and church musicians alike. No sooner had they got used to sometimes nerve-wrecking new forms of worship smacking of trivial entertainment, than a youthful thirst for tradition seems to be the liturgical aroma of the day. Meet the Millennials who are succeeding the Baby Boomers and the GenExers. The Millennials are young people born between 1981 and 2000. "They are called that way because they will presumably live most of their lives in the new millennium," explained Robert Olsavicky, an organist and graduate student at Duquesne University in Pittsburgh. Olsavicky has become a specialist of the roller-coaster changes in worship preferences, changes that parallel developments in society at large. According to Olsavicky, today's young Christians often desire the exact opposite of what the Rev. Rick Warren, a Californian church growth promoter, preaches. Warren shouts at fellow pastors, "Why are you still using that pipe organ people hate?"
>
> "What is happening in the religion of teenagers is nothing short of astounding," wrote Robert Webber in the current issue of *Reformed Worship*, a theological journal. "They want to return to a more stable time, a period of tradition. Not the tradition of the fifties, but of a much earlier time, the tradition of the

old, very old times." ...He sees in the "tradition emerging among the Millennials, Generation X and some Boomers a tradition of classical Christianity filtered through the grid of postmodern, Post-Christian, neo-pagan society." Olsavicky...concurred: "They are looking back to the Reformation era."

In his article, Webber quoted a youth director: "What appeals to this new generation is the cathedral and the stained-glass window. Take the pews out, let them sit on the floor, burn incense, have Scripture readings, lots of music, chants even, and have communion, and they say 'Wow, this is me.'"

Webber reminded his readers that sociologist Francis Fukuyama called the period between 1960 and 1990 "the great disruption," a shift from modernity to post-modernity. Webber added, "The Millennials appear to be the first generation of people coming out of the other side of the crises."[26]

One of our sons is representative of the above description. He's a surveyor by day and a popular music band member by night, a drummer living in Philadelphia. But when it comes to worship, he has said he doesn't want a free-for-all experience, rock music, or even some of the other more recent musical expressions, many of which have little or poor theological content. He wants worship expressions to be different from other kinds in the world. He wants worship to be special, unique, different, and distinct, in a word, holy, like God and what we are called to be. In light of these findings and descriptions, it would be valuable, I believe, to consider what the scripture means and how it may be related to our worshiping today when it says: "...worship the Lord in the splendor of his holiness" (Ps. 29:2). That interpretation and exploration will have to wait for another time.

Pursuing the subject further, if worship should be biblical, then the subject and the object of our worship should be God, with Jesus as a primary focus. In other words, the attention should be not so much on "I" and "me," but rather on "You" ("Thou"). In an article in the March/April 2003 issue of *Moody* magazine, Carolyn Arends, a young

---

[26]Quoted from an internet generated UPI article, April 18, 2002.

Ordering Worship

mother, singer-songwriter with six CD's to her credit, emphasized the point. She told of a time when she had been shopping for a birthday card for her husband. I will let her speak for herself.

> I found cards that described my love for my husband in considerable depth--cards that proclaimed my undying devotion, my quiet contentment, my excitement about the future, my enduring passion, etc. They cast my ability to love in quite a favorable light. The only problem was, it wasn't my birthday. It all felt a little too self-congratulatory, and rather beside the point. All I needed was a card that said "You are a great husband" or "I've never seen a more patient father."...On the way home, I tuned in the local praise-and-worship station. I didn't recognize the first song, but the gist of the lyric was "I really love you Lord and I want to feel your presence," and I could relate. The next song (my favorite) was more along the lines of "I haven't loved you like I should but I'm going to, I promise." The third was more of a proclamation: "I love you Lord, and I always will," set to an exuberant beat.
>
> Maybe it was just a fluke, encountering those three songs on my way home from my ill-fated greeting card excursion. But by the fourth song, I really began to wonder if the modern worship music movement (of which I have been an enthusiastic part) isn't a bit susceptible to an "aren't-I-good-at-loving-you-and-isn't-it-interesting-how-I-love-you-and-enough-about-you-let's-talk-about-my-love-for-you" trap.
>
> It's late. My husband's gift is wrapped and his insufficient card has been signed. The kids are asleep, finally. And I am finding myself drawn to that remarkable passage in Revelation (specifically chapters 4 and 5) that unveils what worship really looks like...they never stop saying: "*Holy, holy, holy is the Lord God Almighty, who was, and is, and is to come*" (4:8). There are 24 elders, too, who fall down to worship every time the living creatures worship and who say: "*You are worthy our Lord and God,*

to receive glory and honor and power, for you created all things, and by your will they were created and have their being" (4:11). And then a Lamb, "looking as if it had been slain," appears in the center of the throne, and a new song begins. *"You are worthy to take the scroll and to open its seals, because you were slain, and with your blood you purchased men for God from every tribe and language and people and nation. You have made them to be a kingdom and priests to serve our God, and they will reign on the earth"* (5:9-10). By the end of the account, "thousands upon thousands" of angels, and "every creature in heaven and on earth and under the earth and on the sea, and all that is in them" are singing: *"To him who sits on the throne and to the Lamb be praise and honor and glory and power, for ever and ever"* (5:13).

I want to be one of the voices in that song of worship--a song that has always been and will always be because it flows to and from the one who sits on that throne and always will. And so I am praying for deliverance from "greeting card worship" ...[And] I am praying for deliverance from my own obsession with self...[27]

Some people have asked me: "Given your views of worship, do you think there is room for what may be called Contemporary services of worship?" By all means, yes! Let me explain. Worship is usually designed and enacted based on the culture within which it is offered, whether in America, Africa, Asia, South America or in jungle tribal settings; whether in a particular ethnic culture, or a sub-culture such as college students. Needless to say, because in today's American culture there are so many people who have no church experience or understanding, it is right that we employ any alternate worship expressions which communicate effectively. Problems I observe include the following. Some people, particularly pastors want to throw out everything that an existing congregation has had in its worship practice in order to try to relate to

---

[27]Carol Arends, "Greeting-Card Worship," *Moody* (March/April 2003, Vol. 102, No. 4), 76.

and reach the un-churched younger generations, and polarization occurs in congregations, even divisions. It takes much wisdom, worship and music sense, and yes even common sense to help shape the course of an existing congregation. As churches grow and there seem to be sufficient numbers to warrant an additional service with more contemporary modes of expression, by all means they should be offered.

Another problem, as I see it, is that pastors say to worship teams, "Go for it," providing little guidance regarding how the service should be shaped. There is a need for pastors to teach what God's written Word says about ordering services of worship whatever the modes of expression. That's doing things by the Book, God's way. Or have some clergy decided all of a sudden that in this area of ministry we no longer have to go by the Book? Unfortunately many Free Church tradition pastors have not done their homework or cared to do it regarding what the Bible says about worship. This is so sad, because worship is so important in church life every single week.

Besides guarding against polarization in existing churches, teaching worship order to those participating in Contemporary services is also needed, appropriate and valuable because some day some of those folks are going to mature spiritually in a variety of ways, and they are going to want something more. A case in point is a remark expressed to me my one of the worship team leaders at Eagles' Nest Christian Fellowship in Peru, Indiana. I invited their worship team to participate in our District Conference worship service. At first they said yes, but later retracted their decision because of the lack of sufficient time after a workday to arrive in time. That is understandable. However, in the course of my conversation with the Eagles' Nest spokesperson, he said to me: "Well, you know, I've been doing this, which I enjoy, for some time now, but I really want something more." People cannot survive indefinitely on infant formula, they have to progress to solid food, whatever that means in this case, as it says in Hebrews 5:13-14.

So there is a place for more than one worship expression based on the needs of people, where they are in their spiritual journey. And to be sure, the Traditional worship of the future will most likely have a different "look" than the Traditional worship of twenty years ago or today.

CLASSIC WORSHIP

I don't believe there needs to be a debate whether or not to have Blended or Contemporary services in churches. The needs exist. The point I wish to make is that pastors have an obligation to teach what the Bible reveals about ordering services of worship, whatever the approach or style employed. Elements may be rendered and communicated or cast differently; but worship still must include a balance of *adoration, confession, pardon, proclamation, and dedication*; because some day people in one type of service may desire to shape their services differently or even participate in another type of worship experience. Knowing what God's intentions are for worshiping will help bridge any gaps and provide common ground for people. It may even make it possible for some to be willing to have their fellow believers offer worship in a mode with which they are not familiar. *So long as the basics of worship order are present and understood, there is a greater chance in long-established churches for parishioner flexibility and acceptance of changes. To do otherwise is unfair, unwise and invites unnecessary conflicts.*

Fellow Christians, we really need to examine what we are doing and how we are doing it when we gather for public worship. To be sure, there are many and stimulating ways of "doing" the elements. With video projection equipment, for example, outlines of sermons can be shown to help impress the word in us richly, to paraphrase Colossians 3:16. Video clips can be used as illustrations in sermons. Mini-dramas can be the method of presenting the scripture lesson upon which the sermon is based. There's no limit to the variety of ways the inclusions of worship may be enacted and rendered. Having a substantially biblically informed order of worship doesn't mean worship is unfriendly or irrelevant. If the inclusions of worship are not substantially biblically driven and God-focused, then our worship experiences should be considered questionable.

What characterizes your church's worship? Are you doing worship God's way? Do your orders reflect biblical teaching and the understanding of worshiping exemplified by the early Christians? What's the focus? Is it God-directed primarily or is it largely "I" or "us" directed? Is there a balance of head and heart (1 Cor. 14:15)? Are you living up to your potential as churches in your worship ministry? We need to be *intentional* about what we do in public worship; and it should be *biblical*.

Other Characteristics of Worship

John Stott's other two named characteristics of worship, which I will mention briefly, are that worship should be *congregational* and *incarnational*. Let me remind us that one New Testament worship term, *leitourgía* (Acts 13:2), suggests that worship is to be offered *by the people*. It is the term from which we derive the word *liturgy*, meaning today *worship order*, an order offered and enacted as much as possible *by the people*. In other words, there should be as much congregational participation as possible, not just for the singing of congregational song literature, but also in group prayers, responsive and/or unison readings of scripture, affirmations of faith; in other words, through *speaking* as well as *singing*. Worship is not intended to be a spectator sport, unless of course we think of God as the spectator. The church, the called-out-ones (*ekklesía*) must resist allowing music and the trends of the casual, sports-minded, spectator-oriented dominant culture to shape our worship orders and inclusions. *God's* word should be our influence. Worship should be *biblically informed* and it should be *congregationally designed*.

Worship services should also be *incarnationally* intended. The Word became flesh, and the written Word is intended to be applied to our lives. Effective use of the arts and technology aids will help make the content of the elements breathe and relate. All elements of the service should be integrated, driven by the scripture base of the sermon of the day, emphasizing what it is which may apply to the lives of the parishioners. The scripture, the sermon, the music, the prayers, every aspect of the service of the day should be designed with the intended learning of the day. In so doing, worship will be *incarnational*.

Values of Worship Orders

Before we leave this subject, let's articulate what are some of the *values of worship orders*. First, in addition to being a vehicle for the local collection of believers to offer worship regularly, the worship order is intended to *model what we should do in our personal lives*. What we do publicly together in worship is a huge reminder and a rehearsal of what we should do privately: praise God; confess our sins; pay attention to

God's written word, learning and applying his truths to our lives; and offer regularly ourselves anew to the Spirit's sway.

Second, a well-crafted worship order should also model our prayer life. In our prayers we should praise the Lord for all his goodness, confess our sins, petition for the needs of others and ourselves, and make expression of dedication. It is interesting to note that the Anglicans have recognized the relationship between worship order and personal prayers by calling their daily worship services Morning and Evening Prayer.

Third, biblically informed worship orders provide individual and collective spiritual stability. Because there is so much instability in the world, regularity of worship order provides home base for people, stability of belief through stability of approach and content. In a world which is out-of-order, we in the church must exemplify order, God's order, doing things God's way. Only then can order out of chaos come to peoples' lives. One of the primary ways of accomplishing that is providing a biblically informed order of worship each week.

Fourth, the order of worship enables the content to be reinforced. I believe the content of the worship elements, as they are presented below, that is, as they are practiced in Burlington, should be Word-driven. As mentioned above with regard to worship being incarnational, the content of the sermon should inform the content of the prayers and the selection of music. Order and integration go hand in hand. When parishioners leave such a service, they will actually have an idea as to what was presented, and learning will be fostered. It will be a more satisfying and meaningful experience. The order serves to impress and instill.

Fifth, the kind of biblically informed worship order given here fosters the full range of attitudes and emotions appropriate and desirable for Christian expression. They mirror and relate to the full rage of emotions we experience in life: such as joy, penitence, longing, sincerity, resolve and the like; all contributing to shaping disciplined lives under God.

Sixth, the worship order serves to unite believers, developing oneness of fellowship and purpose, uniting all into a cohesive whole, a unity without which the work of Christ will not be enjoined. Robert

Webber has said: "Worship will form the community into the image of its content."[28] If the order and content are weak, guess what??????

Are your churches worshiping biblically, congregationally, incarnationally? Pastors, are your worship designs and content guided by the scriptures and the example of the early church? Is worship a priority for you? It should be, because the worship service is *the* primary event for the people of God *every* week. We're not called to plan for the lowest common denominator. We're called to feed the sheep, stretch the sheep, challenge the sheep, and model feeding before the sheep. Our worship services, their orders and content, reveal how much we are intent on doing things God's way.

Historic Influences

Christian worship did not develop overnight or without various influences. We may be reminded that the first Christians were Jews who were used to worshiping God and studying his sacred writings in Temple and Synagogue. Therefore, it is understandable why over time aspects and elements of both settings would become a part of the Christian worshiping experience. Especially since the Temple was destroyed in 70 A.D. we may realize that what took place in the synagogue, particularly the reading and exposition of the Scriptures, and various types and uses of prayers, were naturally carried over into the worship patterns of the early Christians. Acts 17:2, for example, says: "As his custom was, Paul went into the synagogue, and on three Sabbath days he reasoned with them from the Scriptures, explaining and proving that the Christ had to suffer and rise from the dead" (see also Lk. 4:16, Col. 4:16, 1 Th. 5:27, 1 Tim. 4:13). Scripture readings, the singing of psalms and hymns (1 Cor. 14:26, Eph. 5:19, Col. 3:16), common prayers (Acts 2:42, 1 Tim. 2:1-2) with the peoples' Amen (1 Cor. 14:16), sermons (Acts 2:7, 17:1-4, 1 Cor. 14:26, 2 Tim. 4:2), confessions of faith (1 Cor. 15:1-4, 1 Tim. 6:12), and offerings (Rom. 15:26, 1 Cor. 16:1-2, 2 Cor. 9:10-13), were all carried over from synagogue practice to early Christian worship.

---

[28]Robert Webber, "Shaped By Our Worship," *Worship Leader* (January/February 2003, Vol. 12, No. 1), 10.

The unique Christian addition, of course, was the observance of the Lord's Supper (Lk. 22:19-20, Jn. 13, 1 Cor. 10:6, 11:23-26). A *prayer of thanksgiving* for the bread and the cup as remembrances of our Lord's sacrifice accompanied the observance. From this prayer is derived the term *Eucharist*, from the Greek *eucharistía* meaning thanksgiving, a term used by many Christian traditions for the partaking of the bread and the cup.

In early Christian worship patterns we find prayers of intercession (John 17), the praying of the Lord's Prayer (Mt. 6:9-13, Lk. 11:2-4), singing (Mk. 14:26, 1 Cor. 14:26), and the kiss of peace (Rom. 16:16, 1 Cor. 16:20, 1 Pet. 5:14). Worship was held daily (Acts 2:42f, 5:42), on the first day of the week (Acts 20:7, 1 Cor. 16:2), at which time the bread and the cup were shared. By the year 140 or so, as described by the Christian philosopher Justin (c.100-c.165, martyred sometime between 156 and 165), Sunday worship consisted of an order which included some of the elements and influences mentioned above. That order is given in the note below.[29] From this historical record and oth-

---

[29] Justin Martyr's well-known account of Sunday worship in Rome was given in his *Apology* (@140-150), cited here from William D. Maxwell's *An Outline of Christian Worship* (London: Oxford University Press, 1965), 12-13. It included:

The Liturgy of the Word
Readings
Instruction/Exhortation on the Readings
Common Prayers in Litany Form
Psalms and Hymns

The Liturgy of the Upper Room
Kiss of Peace
Offering: Collection of gifts for the poor; bringing in the elements (gifts)
Prayer of Consecration (Eucharistic Prayer):
   Thanksgiving for creation and redemption;
   Memorial of Christ's passion (Anamnesis);
   Oblation of gifts with self-oblation;
   Invocation of the word and the Holy Spirit to bless the gifts of bread and
     wine (Epiclesis);
   Intercessions
   People's Amen.
Fraction
Communion
Dismissal

ers which could be cited, we may say safely, that by around 150 an order of worship was becoming standardized. "The day of the spontaneously offered worship in which all the members of the congregation share at will (as in 1 Cor. 14) is over..."[30] We also know from the instruction manual, *The Didache*, dating from perhaps @100, that an order for the service of Holy Communion integrated a common meal with the Eucharist.[31] There were two streams of practice regarding the inclusion of the Eucharist which developed side by side.

Given at the close of the chapter is a listing of the *theological categories* for a biblically informed order of worship, along with a listing of the *service elements* suggested in scripture and practiced by Christian churches through the centuries. Included are two *sample worship orders, a classic order* as practiced in the Brethren church in Burlington, Indiana, and a suggested *contemporary order* utilizing the classic principles of worship design.

For those who may be uneasy regarding the use of the term *liturgy*, please be aware that every service of worship has a liturgy. That is what we refer to as the *order* of the inclusions of the service. Some church traditions, such as Roman Catholic, Greek Orthodox, Episcopal and Lutheran, have liturgies/orders prescribed by their denominations. Others, such as Methodist and Presbyterian, have suggested and preferred orders. In most Free Church traditions such as Baptists and the Brethren, there are no prescribed orders; yet they still have them, and in that sense the Brethren worship may be described as *liturgical*, especially when we consider the rituals of the baptismal and Holy Communion observances.[32] It may be argued, therefore, that Brethren

---

[30] Ralph P. Martin, *Worship in the Early Church* (Grand Rapids: Wm. B. Eerdmans Publishing, 1964; reprinted 2000), 139.

[31] *The Didache*, also known as "The Teaching of the Twelve Apostles," was a manual of instruction for lay people, particularly those becoming Christians. Sections 9, 10, and 14 speak to the practice of Holy Communion with Section 10 indicating the practice of the Agape Meal. *The Didache* is given in *Ancient Christian Writers*, trans. by James A. Kleist (New York: The Newman Press, 1948), 19-23. A fine discussion of *The Didache* is given in Lucien Deiss, *Springtime of the Liturgy* (Liturgical Texts of the First Four Centuries), trans. by Matthew J. O'Connell (Collegeville, Minnesota: The Liturgical Press, 1979), 73.

[32] *The Brethren Encyclopedia* Volume 2, 1373.

are more liturgical than most Christian bodies. The primary matter here, however, is to have well thought out, biblically informed, and theologically sensible orders of service.

When we unite the understandings of the purposes of worship (glorifying God and strengthening the family of faith), the characteristics of worship (biblical, congregational, and incarnational), the influences from Synagogue and early Christian practices (reading and preaching of God's written Word, common prayers, singing, etc.), the order suggested in Isaiah 6 and elsewhere (e.g. Luke 24 which suggests a word and sacrament combination), and the evidence of known early Christian liturgies, we gain an appreciation for the kinds of things which should take place in corporate worship. The placement of the sermon, for example, makes the most sense before offering and dedication because after the Word is proclaimed then the people respond with the offering of their lives and their tangible expressions of commitment.

Ordering Worship

Order of Worship Guide

Isaiah 6:1-8, Psalm 29:1-2, 1 Corinthians 14:26 & 40
Scriptures given below are either the biblical basis for the worship elements, or they are examples of them.

Theological Categories with Service Elements

PREPARATION – Ps. 100:4, Acts 2:46, 5:42, 1 Cor. 16:2, Rev. 1:10
Prelude/Gathering Music – 1 Chr. 16:4-7, 2 Chr. 5:12-13, Ps. 29:2, Ps. 100
Welcome & Church Concerns
[Kiss of Peace – Rom. 16:16]
Choral/Vocal Solo Introit – Ps. 24:1-2, 27:1-2, 29:1-2, 46:1, 47:1-2

ADORATION – Ps. 22:22, Isa. 6:3-7, Heb. 2:12
Call to Worship – Ps. 29:1-2, 95:1-7, 100 (all)
Hymn – Ps. 100:2, 1 Cor. 14:26, Eph. 5:19, Col. 3:16
Invocation – Ps. 5:7-8, 25:1-3 & 4-6, 84:1-2 & 4, Jn. 14:25-26
Prayer of Confession – Ps. 51:1-12, Isa. 6:5
Words of Assurance – Isa. 6:7, 1 Cor. 14:16 (Amen), Rev. 4:11, 5:12, 7:12
Gloria Patri – Ps. 86:12, Ps. 96:3, Gal. 1:5, Eph. 1:3

PROCLAMATION – Acts 17:2, 2 Cor. 14:26, 1 Th. 5:27, 1 Tim. 4:13
Old Testament Lesson – Acts 17:2, Col. 4:16
Anthem/Vocal Solo – 1 Chr. 15:12-22, 16:4-36. 2 Chr. 5:11-14
New Testament Lesson – Acts 17:2
Sermon – Acts 17:2, 2 Tim. 4:2, Heb. 3:13
Affirmation of Faith – 1 Cor. 15:1-4, Phil. 2:5-11, 1 Tim. 6:2, Heb. 13:15

DEDICATION – Isa. 6:8, Rom. 12:1
Hymn – 1 Cor. 14:26, Col. 3:16
Anthem/Vocal Solo – Ezra 3:65, Neh. 13:10
[Baptism – Mt. 28:19-20, Rom. 6]
Prayer of Intercession – Jn. 14:6, Rom. 8:26-27, 1 Tim. 2:1, Heb. 7:25
The Lord's Prayer – Mt. 6:9-13, Lk. 11:1-4
Offering/Offertory – Ps. 50:14, Pr. 3:9-10, Mic. 6:8, Mal. 3:10, 1 Cor. 16:2
Doxology – Rom. 11:36, Gal. 1:5, Eph. 1:3, Phil. 4:20, Rev. 4:11, 5:12, 7:12
[Holy Communion – Mt. 26:26-28, Lk. 24:27-32, 1 Cor. 11:17-34, Jn. 13]
Prayer of Thanksgiving – Ps. 100:4, 1 Cor. 10:16, Phil. 4:6, 1 Tim. 2:1

CLASSIC WORSHIP

CONCLUSION – Mk. 14:26, 1 Cor. 15:58
Hymn – Mk. 14:26, 1 Cor. 14:26
Benediction – Num. 6:24-26, Ps. 67:1-2, Rom. 15:13, 1 Cor. 15:58,
  2 Cor. 13:14, Eph. 3:20-21, Phil. 4:7, 1 Tim. 1:17, 1 Th. 5:23,
  Heb. 13:20-21, Jude 24-25
Postlude/Dismissal Music – Ps. 150

Classic Order

GATHERING MUSIC
Prelude, Hymns & Choruses

WELCOME AND CHURCH CONCERNS

CALL TO WORSHIP (Adapted from Ruth 2:4)
Pastor: The Lord be with you.
People: And also with you.
Pastor: Lift up your hearts.
People: We lift them up to the Lord.

*HYMN   "Come, All Christians, Be Committed"

*INVOCATION

*PRAYER OF CONFESSION (All):
Gracious God, we stand before you a people who desire to be faithful. We long for increase in our church, both spiritually and numerically. Yet too often we hold back the effort needed for genuine progress. Sometimes it is due to slothfulness, sometimes because we wish to have our own way, other times because we just don't know how to proceed. Please forgive us for absence of vision, for lack of fervor, for ignorance and pride. Cause us to be resolved to think of you and the work of Christ first, and others next. Help us to set aside personal ambition and perhaps even preference, and to work truly for the welfare of the Church of our Lord: in whose name we pray. Amen.

*WORDS OF ASSURANCE

READINGS   Nehemiah 8:1-12, Acts 2:37-47

MUSIC (Solo/Ensemble/Choir)

SERMON   "Living Up to Our Potential in Ministry"

*HYMN   "Take My Life" (Sing Stanzas 1, 2; Speak 3, 4, Sing 5, 6)

Ordering Worship

PRAYER OF INTERCESSION/THE LORD'S PRAYER (Debts}

OFFERING/OFFERTORY/*DOXOLOGY

PRAYER OF THANKSGIVING (All):
Gracious God, we thank you for the prompting from your word, for the nudges and the leading. Help us to understand the needs of ministry, and to continue to offer ourselves and our resources for the advancement of your work: for the sake of Jesus Christ our Lord, and for the souls of many. Amen.

*HYMN   "Higher Ground"

*BENEDICTION & DISMISSAL MUSIC
  [* Asterisks mean please stand.]

Contemporary Order

GATHERING MUSIC
(Beginning @ 15 Minutes Before the Hour; Recorded Instrumental CD Music (@ 10 Min.); Familiar Songs with Projected Words (@ 5 Min. Before the Hour).

WELCOME/CONCERNS (@ 3 Min.)

OPENING PRAYER (@ 1 Min.)
Perhaps Prefaced with a Responsive, Four Line Scripture
Call to Worship, Projected.

SONGS & HYMNS (@ 7 Min. Projected)

CONFESSION (@ 3 Min.)
Silent Prayer, followed by Group Confession (based on sermon topic; projected); Followed by Leader's Statement of God's Forgiveness with scripture sentence.

READING/PRESENTATION (@ 4 Min.)
May be a mini-drama of it, or several persons sharing it in dramatic reading style.

SPECIAL MUSIC (@ 4 Min.)
Solo/Ensemble/Worship Team/ etc.

SERMON (@ 20-25 Min.)
May have a mini-drama or video clips as illustrations. Sermon outline projected.

CLASSIC WORSHIP

QUESTIONS & RESPONSES (@ 7 Min.)
After the sermon, at placed microphones persons may ask questions for clarification or further information.

SONGS FOR AFFIRMATION (@ 5 Min.)
Selected according to the application from the sermon.

PRAYERS (@ 7 Min.) For needs of the Body & Others; Silent Prayer; Three or four persons will pray by prior invitation and readiness.

COLLECTION (@ 3 Min.)
Rather than have a basket at back of the room, educate the folks that offering is a response to the spoken word.

DOXOLOGY Contemporary Setting

SONGS/HYMNS with INVITATION TO COMMITMENT

CLOSING PRAYER

DISMISSAL MUSIC Live or Recorded

Chapter Five
Praying in Worship

One of the values, as well as one of the beauties and benefits of the *order of worship* practiced generally throughout the history of the Church, and as given in the previous chapter, is that it is intended to mirror, model, teach, and hopefully encourage the use of an appropriate *outline for our private praying*. We should begin our personal prayers with expressions of *adoration*; praising God, especially by mentioning who God is, some of his attributes and some of the things he has done, his providential care. After praise, as we've learned from Isaiah 6, *confession* is to be made. In comparison with God, the only truly Holy One, we humbly bow our hearts, acknowledge our sin, and ask for forgiveness. Only after adoration and confession are we then in a proper spiritual posture to make *intercession* for others as well as make petitions for ourselves. To say this another way, after we have offered praise to God, our provider and redeemer from whom all blessings flow; and after we have expressed genuine repentance and sought God's mercy; only then are we justified to make petitions of our heavenly Father, requests for care for others and ourselves. Following intercessions we should end our prayers with words of *thanksgiving*, a kind of review or summary of God's specific provisions, even previously answered prayers, accompanied by a request for his continued help. The public worship order is intended to model and teach us how we may pray when in private. The point is made with even greater clarity, as mentioned above, when we realize some other traditions such as the Church of England and the Protestant Episcopal Church refer to their worship orders as the Order for Morning Prayer and the Order for Evening Prayer, the term prayer being a synonym for the public worship experience. Both orders are given in their worship guidebooks, named the *Book of Common Prayer*.

Congregational Prayers

This leads us to the primary consideration of this present chapter, namely *congregational prayers* in worship. It has been my observation that in most evangelical churches there is no provision for common prayers; that is, printed prayers which the entire congregation prays together in unison. This is one of the great tragedies of conservative Protestant public worship. Pastors and parishioners think nothing of singing hymns and songs together at the same time. They also take the elements of Holy Communion together at the same time; even say some common words together as they do. They may read the same scripture together as unison or responsive readings. And yet when it comes to praying in worship, many churches leave that up to the pastor or other leaders. The congregation as a whole does not pray together. Some people have the idea that prepared prayers for the group (perhaps even prepared prayers for the pastor) could not be 'spiritual'. It would seem this point of view must have originated as a reaction against certain other Christian traditions which have prescribed liturgies and which congregations also pray the Lord's Prayer together in worship; and that somehow these practices must be inappropriate. In the next chapter we will focus attention on the matter of praying the Lord's Prayer in worship; but for now let us make the plea to consider faithfully the wisdom of providing for common prayers in worship. In the Brethren congregation I serve, they have found the parts of the service in which they participate together, including the common prayers, to be so meaningful, that when on a rare occasion one of them may be omitted for a particular reason or need that day, they feel something is very much missing in their worshiping experience. They have said so.

Let me remind us that the meaning of corporate worship is that which is "the work of the people" (*leitourgía*). Because group worshiping is supposed to be just that, worship offered by a group, then as many of the elements of the service as possible should be offered by the group. Group prayers are corporate contact with God.[33] Corporate worship's intention is to enable the people of God to speak with a common voice, offer common praise, common confession, common intercession, and common thanksgiving. In addition to the need we all have

---

[33]Sue Curran. *The Praying Church: Principles and Power of Corporate Praying* (Lake Mary, FL: Creation House Press, 2001), 76.

as individuals to confess our sins, churches as bodies of believers with common ministries and a collective witness need to make confession for their common faults, shared failures regarding not reaching out to others, or allowing those who desire to be the powerful within the parish to get away with untoward words or behaviors, which only eventually leads to internal disunity within the ranks and mars the image and witness of the congregation as ambassadors of Jesus Christ before their respective communities. We do not live or serve in a void. We live and serve in community, being mutually dependent upon one another, and combining our energies and gifts to further Christ's work. Congregations in worship need to pray together with one voice. In addition, common congregational prayers cultivate a sense of oneness which further enables common ministry thrusts to be accomplished and more effectively. Corporate prayer is intended not only to be the *heart* of the corporate worship experience, it is intended as well to go *through* the order of worship.[34] "The ideal prayer is the voice of the Church."[35] Thus the reasons for the group prayers in the worship orders suggested in the previous chapter. The family of faith praying together in worship is a means for and is an expression of its common life, of its solidarity, of its unified commitment, and of its spiritual fellowship.[36]

Needless to say, we would not be so rigid in our thinking to suggest that there is no place for spontaneous prayers or even those which may be termed extemporaneous after preparation. That is not the point taken or advanced here. What is being emphasized is that there is a lack of understanding by many in the evangelical community regarding public worship planning and ordering and the matter of common congregational praying in worship. The plea is made here to correct both.

The biblical principle which lies behind group praying is the "principle of agreement" taught by our Lord.[37] "Again, I tell you that if two

---

[34] George A. Buttrick. *Prayer* (Nashville: Abingdon-Cokebury Press, 1942), 283.

[35] Henry Ward Beecher. *Yale lectures on Preaching* (New York: Fords, Howard, and Hulbert, 1893), 57.

[36] Franklin M. Segler. *Christian Worship: Its Theology and Practice* (Nashville: Broadman Press, 1967), 111.

[37] Curran, 10.

of you on earth agree about anything you ask for, it will be done for you by my Father in heaven. For where two or three come together in my name, there am I with them" (Mt. 18:19-20). The Greek word translated *agree* is *sumphoneo,* which obviously is suggestive of our word symphony. Collectively, the common prayers by the Body in worship are like a symphony with several movements: praise, confession, intercession and thanksgiving (It might be interesting for a gifted musician to attempt composing a symphony or symphonic choral work with those four movements!). Common prayer in worship is like offering a *concert* of prayer. Our Lord made it perfectly clear that Christians are intended to pray collectively when he instructed his disciples to pray "Our" Father. The plurals in the Lord's Prayer leave no doubt (Our…us…we). If there is anything which should characterize the activity of the worship house it is prayer (Isa. 56:7, Mt. 21:13). Our Brethren heritage is one where congregational prayers have been employed in worship. "Prayers were at one time spontaneous, but later pastors did not hesitate to read classic or original prayers. In some instances printed bulletins included prayers to be prayed in unison by members."[38] For purposes of historical understanding and appreciation, as well as providing guidance for the preparation of congregation-

---

[38]Kenneth I. Morse. "Worship, Public," *The Brethren Encyclopedia*, Volume Two, 1378. For a more thorough discussion of Brethren practices in public worship, see in the same volume of *The Brethren Encyclopedia* the complete articles for "Worship, public," 1373-1379; "Prayer," 1051-1053; "Preaching," 1053-1054; and "Music," 898-900. These will lead the reader to many other sources as given in the bibliographic citations at the close of each article, such as: Martin Grove Brumbaugh, *A History of the German Baptist Brethren in Europe and America* (Mount Morris, IL: Brethren Publishing House, 1899), 155-160; H. R. Holsinger, *Holsinger's History of the Tunkers and The Brethren Church* (Oakland, CA: Pacific Press Publishing Co., 1901), 239-255; James H. Lehman, *The Old Brethren* (New York: Pillar Books, 1976), 93-135; William G. Willoughby, *Counting the Cost: The Life of Alexander Mack 1679-1735* (Elgin, IL: The Brethren Press, 1979), 61-76. See also Donald Durnbaugh, "Brethren Worship and Polity," *Fruit of the Vine: A History of the Brethren 1708-1995* (Elgin, Illinois: Brethren Press, 1997), 103-126; Kenneth I. Morse, *Move in Our Midst* (Elgin, IL: The Brethren Press, 1977), 46-67; Dale R. Stoffer, *Background and Development of Brethren Doctrine 1650-1987* (Philadelphia, PA: The Brethren Encyclopedia, Inc., 1989), 99-102 and other citations on worship in the Index.

al prayers, it will be useful to discuss the type of prayer which several Christian traditions have included in their worship orders for centuries: the *collect*.

The Model of the Collect

One of the classic and oft-quoted collects is the following, adapted here from *The Book of Common Prayer* (1662, Oxford University Press).

> Almighty God, unto whom all hearts are open, all desires known, and from whom no secrets are hid; cleanse the thoughts of our hearts by the inspiration of your Holy Spirit, that we may perfectly love you, and worthily magnify your holy name: through Jesus Christ our Lord. Amen.

The collect may be thought of as having three or five parts. The three-part form can be described as having an *Address* (Almighty God, unto whom all hearts are open, all desires known, and from whom no secrets are hid); the *Petition* (cleanse the thoughts of our hearts by the inspiration of your Holy Spirit, that we may perfectly love you, and worthily magnify your holy name); and the *Conclusion* (through Jesus Christ our Lord. Amen).

A more complete analysis of the collect as a five-part form yields the following:

1. The Address: "Almighty God"

2. Attributes of God or More About the Focus of the Address: "unto whom all hearts are open, all desires known, and from whom no secrets are hid"

3. The Petition: "Cleanse the thoughts of our hearts by the inspiration of your Holy Spirit"

4. The Purpose of the Petition: "that we may perfectly love you, and worthily magnify your holy name"

5. The Conclusion: "through Jesus Christ our Lord. Amen."

CLASSIC WORSHIP

In some traditions the collect is a prayer offered by the pastor or priest with the congregation saying the Amen only. Louis Weil explains:

> The fact that the collect is spoken by a bishop or priest who is presiding at a particular liturgy in no way diminishes the corporate significance of the prayer. Rather, it is a potent reminder that the prayer of the ordained leader of the assembly is linked to the role of the ordained person to pray *in the name of the church*. The "Amen" of the people is its corporate ratification: the collect is the summary of *their* prayer.[39]

In addition to the principle of agreement being scriptural ground for group prayers in worship, we may also appreciate the format of the prayer of Peter and John in Acts 4:24-30 as biblical precedent and example of the collect type of prayer. Notice the parts of the prayer.

The Address: "Sovereign Lord" (v. 24)

Attribute/Work of God: "you made heaven and the earth and the sea, and everything in them. You spoke by the Holy Spirit through the mouth of your servant, our father David ... (etc.)" (vv. 24-28)

The Petition: "Now, Lord, consider their threats and enable your servants to speak your word with great boldness. Stretch out your hand to heal and perform miraculous signs and wonders..." (vv. 29-30)

The Purpose: [Implied; that their speaking, the healings and the miraculous signs would bring glory to God, others might become believers, and the church unified; see v. 32]

The Conclusion: "through the name of your holy servant Jesus."

The reader may say, well that's all well and good for those churches and clergy in the more prescribed-liturgical communities; that's not for

---

[39]Louis Weil. *Gathered to Pray: Understanding Liturgical Prayer* (Cambridge, Mass: Crowley Publications, 1986), 38-39.

us. We must disagree with that criticism. First, pastors in our churches usually offer an *Opening Prayer*, otherwise referred to as an *Invocation*. The collect form offers a superb example of the kind of format one may employ for the *Invocation*. Moreover, it is our contention here that pastors should be so God-honoring and hold the worship hour in such high regard, that they prepare well for this most significant gathering in the life of the local Body of believers each week; that means thinking about and being prepared for all aspects of the service, including the prayers. The collect form serves well to assist pastors and other worship leaders to know what kinds of matters to include in an Invocation. One brief example might be something similar to the following.

Address: "Gracious God,"

Words About God: "you who have loved us from ages past and put in motion your plan of redemption,"

Petition: "meet with us in this hour through the presence of your Holy Spirit,"

Purpose: "that we may worthily magnify your Holy Name; that we may give you the sincere thanks of our hearts; and that we may be strengthened in faith:"

Conclusion: "through Jesus Christ our Lord we pray. Amen."

A second value of being aware of the collect form is to know how to prepare appropriately for group prayer in worship. While collects historically have not always been prayed entirely by congregations, it is our contention that in Protestant and evangelical churches where we say we take seriously the notion of the Church as the *Body* of Christ and as a *priesthood of all believers*, the more the Body participates, the more the priesthood of believers offers the elements of worship, the more genuine is the worship which they offer as "the work of the people." The collect form can assist pastors as they prepare congregational prayers of confession and thanksgiving which are printed in the bulletin at the appropriate locations within the service. For example, a congregational *Prayer of Confession* might be:

Address: "Heavenly Father,"

Words About God: "you who have offered your only Son as a sacrifice of atonement for our sins,"

Petition: "we pray for your mercy and forgiveness, for we have fallen far short of your intentions for us; we have sinned in thought, word and deed. Cleanse our lives by the power of the blood of Christ, and fill us with the presence and guiding influence of your Holy Spirit,"

Purpose: "that we may more effectively mirror the character of Christ before others, so that others will be drawn to faith in Jesus."

Conclusion: "We pray in his name. Amen."

The more we do with one voice, the more appropriate is our gathering for worship. We sing together. There's no defensible reason why we should not pray together as well. Less spectator and entertainment-oriented, and more participation and prayer-patterned worship is what is needed. In addition, we strongly suggest all of the group prayers in the worship order include ideas supportive of those given in the sermon of the day. In that way the topic of that's day's worship may be enhanced and instilled more thoroughly; and the whole worshiping experience will be more unified and meaningful. *Let's have Congregational Prayers in our worship services!* Their importance cannot be overstated. In well-designed worship they are "a kind of microcosm of the underlying framework of the entire [worship order],"[40] and as mentioned above they serve to remind us of the parts of the prayers we should offer in our private devotions.

Pastoral Leadership in Prayer

Having said all of the above, it remains that some will ask: What should the Pastor do regarding prayers in worship? To be sure, the pastor or other worship leader will offer an *Invocation/Opening Prayer*, a prayer to request (invoke) the Spirit of God to be present, and to ask

---
[40]Weil, 32.

that he enable all which will be offered during the service be for his glory and the edification of the gathered family of faith.

During the time of the *Prayer of Confession,* while we believe strongly the Body gathered should offer a common prayer (different each week based if possible on some aspect of the sermon theme), it would be meaningful before the pastor leads the parishioners in that prayer to allow for a time of silence where all gathered have an opportunity to offer their personal words of confession to God. Again, it has been my observation that there are very few evangelical churches within the Free Church traditions which have any provision for confession by the people in public worship. This is absolutely wrong; it is unbiblical; and should be corrected. A congregational prayer of confession and/or an opportunity for parishioners to pray silently are ways this may be accomplished.

In many churches the pastor or other leader offers a prayer during the time when the offering is taken. Along with what we have been saying above, it is the view taken here that this prayer may better be offered by the congregation as a *Prayer of Thanksgiving.* After all, it is their tithes and offerings which are being presented. Following the actual receiving of them, a congregational prayer of thanksgiving would include expression of gratitude for God's blessings and a word of dedicating the gifts to God's work. The thanksgiving part of the prayer may include as well a remark regarding our appreciation for the specific provisions of God which may have been mentioned in the sermon. In this way the teaching of the day will be reinforced, thus making the prayer as a whole even more purposeful and the sermon content even more applicable.

For the time of the *Prayer of Intercession,* pastors and parishioners have differing views regarding whether or not to ask the congregation for any concerns which may be included in the prayer, or if anyone other than the pastor should pray; because, while all concerns are valuable to individuals and to God, within the worship setting it is more appropriate to mention the more serious matters rather than what could be viewed as minor concerns; and some persons who might wish to pray have a tendency to go on forever or preach as they pray without regard for the needs of the occasion. Wisdom, common sense, and the particular church's circumstances or desires need to be considered. As for my experience, I have usually asked if there are any concerns. Then I offer a prayer which includes my pre-thought matters followed by extemporaneous praying for the concerns which were shared. In some instances in the past I have asked parishioners who have a concern to write it out on a card and give it to me personally before the service, or request an usher to deliver the message. The Prayer of Intercession time is concluded with the congregation praying the Lord's Prayer. Again, in the next chapter we will speak specifically regarding the values of regular praying of the Lord's Prayer in worship.

In the vast majority of more conservative and evangelical churches it has been the practice for the pastor to offer a *Pastoral Prayer*. In light of the teaching given in this volume, the Pastoral Prayer as it is traditionally conceived and which actually historically speaking is a more recent inclusion in Protestant worship orders is really unnecessary if the worship order is biblically sound, the people are doing their parts of the service, and there is a pastor-led Prayer of Intercession.

The *Pastoral Prayer*, having been referred to as the main prayer of the worship service, contains the following parts: *adoration, confession, petition, intercession, commitment, and a concluding ascription of praise.*[41] Sound familiar? From my observation, some pastors will include a statement of invocation. This is most interesting since by the time the Pastoral Prayer is offered, the service is half over! And regarding confession, the Body is quite capable of confessing and needs to do so. From our point of view, unless there is a keen sense of agreement by all for what the pastor prays, *our* faults will not be forgiven by God unless *we* confess them.

I will grant that there is a biblical precedent for the priestly office praying to God on behalf of the people. There's no doubt of that, and there are occasions when that may be the best approach. There is a place for the pastor to pray, and we expect pastors to pray. A biblical example of a prayer which may be considered a forerunner and model of a Pastoral Prayer is that which is given in Daniel 9. It is an interest-

---

[41]Segler, 115-116.

ing read. However, I believe, and the Church at large for centuries has believed that the prayers which make the most sense for the pastor to offer are those of Invocation and Intercession. The congregation is quite capable of offering pastor-prepared and printed common prayers for all to pray. That's pastoral leadership at its best, shepherding the flock. The elements suggested above for the Pastoral Prayer are better divided up according to the places in the service which are appropriate.

There are some excellent texts available which present the suitable elements of prayer in general. Both Isaac Watt's (1674-1748) treatise, *So Amazing, So Divine: A Guide to Living Prayer*,[42] and Matthew Henry's *A Method for Prayer*[43] present discussion on the primary subjects for inclusion for a comprehensive prayer. Such literature has guided pastors when learning how to compose and offer a Pastoral Prayer, as well as teach anyone how to pray when in private. Pastors should be educated in such matters. However, if corporate worship orders are what they should be, the areas of prayer are better shared by pastor and people as outlined above. Many pastors may be reluctant to do so because it takes more thought and effort to prepare more thoroughly for corporate worship, including aesthetically pleasing and comprehensive bulletins. These faults need to be corrected, for the weekly worshiping experience is the most important 'event' in the life of the gathered local church. Care is required and is here sincerely encouraged. We're talking about the worship of GOD! He deserves the best biblically-based and biblically-shaped services we can offer.

One word regarding the close of the worship service will conclude this consideration. Pastors also offer a *Benediction*. This is most often a declarative statement, perhaps one of the benedictions given by the Apostle Paul in his letters. Benedictions are not necessarily prayers, therefore. They are statements of blessing and consecration. There's no need for pastors to prompt people to close their eyes and bow their heads when what is said is not a prayer. Needless to say, however,

---

[42]Isaac Watts. *So Amazing, So Divine: A Guide to Living Prayer* (Brewster, Mass.: Paraclete Press, 1997).

[43]Matthew Henry. *A Method for Prayer* (Geanies House, Fearn, Ross-shire, Scotland: Christian Focus Publications, Ltd., 1994).

should a pastor offer a *Closing Prayer* which requests of God that all be blessed, then certainly that is equally appropriate. The point is, for this and for all of the elements and inclusions of corporate worship, pastors should think; what are they and the people doing, when and why.

Chapter Six

Praying the Lord's Prayer

It has been said that the Lord's Prayer is misnamed, that our Lord would not have prayed this prayer because there was no need for him to pray for forgiveness of sins, and that the prayer may be better labeled the Disciples' Prayer.[44] To be sure, Jesus' need would not have been to confess sins, and the prayer was given for disciples to pray. However, the prayer is truly our Lord's instruction. It is the prayer he formulated for those who would follow him. It is, therefore, the prayer which bears his stamp of ownership and authority, and is very appropriately attributed to him as the source of its formulation. That is one reason for it being called the Lord's Prayer.

Since the early church Christians have been praying the Lord's Prayer in public worship. Thomas Aquinas (c.1225-1274) referred to it as the best of all prayers.[45] Nicolas Ayo described the prayer as seminal of all Christian prayer.[46] In the opening remarks of his comprehensive work on the Lord's Prayer, Thomas Watson (1620-1688) described Jesus' words as a "directory for prayer" and a "system or body of divinity."[47] Most Christians would resonate affirmatively with the idea of the prayer being a directory or outline for appropriate prayer. The notion of the Lord's Prayer being an outline for Christian prayer has been accepted generally. John Calvin referred to it as "a prescribed form."[48]

---

[44] For example, Haddon Robinson. *Jesus' Blueprint for Prayer* (Grand Rapids: RBC Ministries, 1989), 3-4.

[45] Thomas Acquinas. *Summa Theologiae* Vol. 39 (New York: McGraw-Hill Book Company, 1964), II, II, 83, 9.

[46] Nicolas Ayo. *The Lord's Prayer: A Survey Theological and Literary* (Notre Dame, Indiana: University of Notre Dame, 1992), 6.

[47] Thomas Watson. *The Lord's Prayer* (Edinburgh: The Banner of Truth Trust, 1993), 1.

[48] John T. McNeill, ed. *Calvin: Institutes of the Christian Religion* (Philadelphia: The Westminster Press, 1960), Vol. 2, III, XX, 34.

CLASSIC WORSHIP

Martin Luther (1483-1546) called it "a brief formula" for prayer.[49] Matthew Henry described it as "a method for praying."[50] More contemporary labels include Frank Stagg's traditional "Model Prayer,"[51] David Jeremiah's "a road map for prayer,"[52] and Max Lucado's "floor plan to our spiritual house."[53]

The Lord's Prayer has had a prominent place in the worship of the Brethren. "By the middle of the 19th century, Brethren public and private worship had become more standardized...A period of prayer in the worship service was to be preceded by a brief exhortation on the purpose and manner of prayer after which all should kneel while several persons pray. Prayers should be concluded by reciting the Lord's Prayer."[54] "Traditional Brethren services encouraged prayer by exhortation to prayer, by permitting deacons and other lay members to pray in public, and by regularly employing the prayer that Jesus gave his disciples."[55]

In our congregation it has been the practice to pray the Lord's Prayer at the close of congregational business meetings and during the Love Feast (Holy Communion). However, as with many congregations, the regular inclusion of the Lord's Prayer in the weekly worship service was non-existent. One would have to believe this is due in part over the years to the transformation of public worship formats brought about by the Revival Movement of the second half of the 19th century, and further by the Charismatic Movement of the second half of the 20th century. Worship influenced by these movements tended to become less

---

[49]Martin Luther. "The Sermon on the Mount: Sermons," *Luther's Works* Vol. 21, Jaroslav Pelikan, ed. (St. Louis: Concordia Publishing House, 1956), 145.

[50]Matthew Henry. *Matthew Henry's Commentary On the Whole Bible* Vol. 5 (Peabody, Mass: Hendrickson Publishers, 1994), 59.

[51]Frank Stagg. "Matthew," *The Broadman Bible Commentary* Vol. 8 (Nashville: Broadman Press, 1969), 115.

[52]David Jeremiah. *Prayer The Great Adventure* (Sisters, Oregon: Multnomah Publishers, Inc., 1997), 69.

[53]Max Lucado. *The Great House of God* (Dallas: Word Publishing, 1997), 7.

[54]Dennis Martin, "Prayer," *The Brethren Encyclopedia* Volume 2, 1051.

[55]Kenneth I. Morse, 1378.

formal and less structured, more evangelistically oriented, with greater emphasis on congregational singing, more exclusively praise-oriented, and with what seems to have been an intentionality to offer a worshiping experience which was divorced from the mainline communities of faith. With that the Lord's Prayer was left out of the weekly worship event. We offer here, therefore, a brief consideration of the values and important potentialities of the congregation praying the Lord's Prayer regularly in public worship.[56]

Collective Use

Another reason for calling it the Lord's Prayer is derived from the Lukan account of the prayer. Luke 11:1 says: "One day Jesus was praying in a certain place. When he finished, one of his disciples [we would love to know which one] said to him, 'Lord, teach us to pray, just as John taught his disciples.'" This is significant because it tells us that it was the custom for rabbis to teach their disciples a prayer which would be uniquely theirs, a kind of mark of identity with that rabbi, and which they might use regularly.[57] Moreover, this understanding helps us realize the prayer was intended for group use. The *plurals* of the prayer tell us directly that the intention of Jesus was for his disciples to pray it together. If Jesus formulated this prayer as one for disciples to pray, then we are instructed and invited by him to pray it as a *mark of our identity* with and allegiance to him. The privilege and the honor are ours to know Jesus himself has given us a prayer to pray. We are united together with the original disciples, with those of all ages since, and presently with all believers from every nation and station in life as we pray together these treasured words.

To be sure, the Lord's Prayer is a guide for praying, or as Michael Youssef termed it, "God's curriculum for Prayer."[58] However, the

---

[56]The present chapter is a revision of the last chapter of Peter E. Roussakis, *United in Prayer: A Guide to Understanding and Praying the Lord's Prayer* (Burlington, IN: Meetinghouse Press, 2006).

[57]William Barclay. *The Gospel of Luke* rev. ed. (Philadelphia: The Westminster Press, 1975), 143.

[58]Michael Youssef. *The Prayer That God Answers: Experiencing the Power and Fullness of The Lord's Prayer* (Nashville: Thomas Nelson Publishers, 2000), 9.

expressed instruction of Jesus was that we actually say the prayer together. The Dutch Reformed theologian Herman Witsius (1636-1708) expounded intensely about this matter in his major treatise on the prayer.

> Undoubtedly, the disciple who made the request did not so much desire to be informed about the manner of praying, as to be furnished with a copy and form of prayer, similar to those which had been given by the Pharisees to their followers, and by John to his hearers. This desire our Lord Jesus cheerfully gratifies, not saying, 'pray nearly in this manner,' but *when ye pray, say*. He does not say, ask that the name of God may be hallowed, that his kingdom may come, and so on,--as he would have done if he had meant it merely as a copy. But he says *when ye pray say, Our Father which art in heaven, hallowed be thy name,* suggesting not the subjects only, or the dispositions, but the words in which our Heavenly Father chooses to be addressed.[59]

To emphasize, Luke 11:2 says (italics added): "He said to them, 'When you pray, *say*......'" Our Lord expects us to say this prayer as his disciples and to pray it together. John Stott concurs: "...he tells us to pray in the plural 'Our Father', and one can scarcely pray that prayer in secret alone."[60] It is clear that Jesus intended the prayer to be prayed by disciples in the group setting and using the words he taught.

Witsius also explained that rabbis taught their people prayers which would encapsulate a body of truth, perhaps a brief compendium of previously presented and more extensive prayers. Such prayers would be used to summarize and conclude longer prayers given by the rabbi.[61] The summary prayer would be prayed by the people, using the exact words the rabbi taught. In today's worship, following an Invocation or

---

[59]Herman Witsius. *Sacred Dissertations on The Lord's Prayer* (Escondido, CA: The den Dulk Christian Foundation, 1994), 126.

[60]John Stott. *The Message of the Sermon on the Mount* (Downers Grove, IL: InterVarsity Press, 1978), 134.

[61]Witsius, 124-125.

Prayer of Intercession offered by the pastor, or as an affirmation of faith, it is appropriate for the congregation to pray the Lord's Prayer.

In ancient church usage, as Witsius points out, it was also customary to pray the Lord's Prayer, after which other prayers might be added.[62] So while its usage is variable, it is clear from the days of Jesus onward, the Lord's Prayer was intended to be prayed by disciples together. Witsius asked: "What prayer can have greater power with the Father than that which came from the lips of the Son, who is the Truth?"[63] We should be ever thankful that Jesus formulated for us a prayer which is uniquely ours and for all Christians, past, present and future.

Values and Potentialities

We may say, therefore, that one of the values and *potentialities of praying the Lord's Prayer in worship* is its *unifying* capacity. Believers in Christ are bonded together in the praying of the prayer our Lord has taught us. Along with Holy Communion and baptism, the Lord's Prayer is truly a symbol of Christian identity and oneness. Praying the prayer together awakens Christians' consciousness to the presence of God, to one another, and to their common bond under our Father in heaven, for it serves as "the key-note of all Christian prayers. It is the concert-pitch of the universal heavenly choir of the whole family on earth and in heaven."[64]

The other remark by Watson cited above, that the Lord's Prayer is "a system or body of divinity," may not be understood by parishioners of any tradition unless a series of sermons or classes were offered explaining the meaning of each phrase of the prayer. Through such ways it may bring to peoples' awareness a dimension of the prayer not previously considered. And it is this aspect of the Lord's Prayer which helps us appreciate a second potentiality of praying it together in worship. Since in each phrase of the prayer there is embodied essential Christian

---

[62]Ibid., 129.

[63]Ibid.

[64]Philip Schaff. *A Christian Catechism for Sunday Schools and Families* (Philadelphia: American Sunday School Union, 1880), 29.

beliefs expressed in petitionary form,[65] praying the prayer is a way of sounding forth the truths contained within it; it is a means of *confessing and proclaiming our faith*.

This second remark by Watson was based on the truth of the prayer's composition and upon a statement of Tertullian (c.150-220), who, in his treatise *De Oratione* ("On Prayer"), called the Lord's Prayer a "compendium of the whole gospel" (breviarium totius evangelii).[66] Other commentators have spoken similarly. Cyprian (200-258) said the Lord's Prayer is a "comprehensive and sublime compend."[67] Luther characterized the trilogy of the Catechism (the Ten Commandments, the Creed, and the Lord's Prayer), as a "digest of doctrine."[68] G. Campbell Morgan (1863-1945) described the prayer as being a part of the "Manifesto of the King,"[69] referring to the Sermon on the Mount of which the Lord's Prayer is a part in Matthew's Gospel. William Willimon and Stanley Hauerwas call it "public theology."[70] Philip Schaff (1819-1893) described the Lord's Prayer as "the gospel in a nutshell."[71] And Nicolas Ayo commented: "The Lord's Prayer is a precis of the whole gospel, the distillation of the substance of the good news."[72]

---

[65]A thorough discussion of the Christian beliefs encapsulated in the phrases of the Lord's Prayer is given in Peter E. Roussakis, *United in Prayer: A Guide to Understanding and Praying the Lord's Prayer* (see note 56).

[66]Watson, 1. "Compendium" is Watson's and Ayo's (p. 5) rendering of Tertullian's "breviarium." "An epitome of the whole Gospel" is the translation given by the Rev. S. Thelwall in *Ante-Nicene Fathers*, Vol. 3, Alexander Roberts & James Donaldson, eds. (Peabody, Mass: Hendrickson Publishers, 1994), 681.

[67]Cyprian. "Elucidation III," *Ante-Nicene Fathers* Vol. 5, Alexander Roberts and James Donaldson, eds. (Peabody, Mass: Henrickson Publishers, 1994), 559.

[68]F. Samuel Janzow. *Luther's Large Catechism* (St. Louis: Concordia Publishing House, 1978), 12.

[69]G. Campbell Morgan. *The Practice of Prayer* (Belfast, Northern Ireland: Ambassador Productions, Ltd, 1995), 57.

[70]William H. Willimon and Stanley Hauerwas. *Lord, Teach Us: The Lord's Prayer and the Christian Life* (Nashville: Abingdon Press, 1996), 17.

[71]Philip Schaff, 29.

[72]Ayo, 6.

The combination of petition as profession was the subject of J. Harold Ellens' fine article, "*Communication Theory and Petitionary Prayer.*" He made the case that by its very nature and composition the Lord's Prayer is a confession of faith. He described the first section of the prayer in Matthew's account as an affirmation by us in prayer of that which God is and does. The second section (vv. 11-13a.) he describes as an affirmation of our human nature as children of God, of the identification of our need for God's redemptive care (e.g. bread [provisions]). It is also a certification of our human need for forgiveness.[73] Section three (v. 13b.) he described as "a doxological summary of all that is affirmed or confessed or celebrated in sections one and two."[74] Ellens suggests, therefore, that the Lord's Prayer is essentially a declarative prayer, a declaratory profession of faith in petitionary formula.[75]

So when we gather together and pray the prayer we do more than offer a collective prayer to God. Without realizing it, we are *confessing our faith*. In the preface of the prayer we announce and affirm our relationship with God, our Father. In the petitions we confess our willingness and desire to hallow God's name, to enter and increase and persevere in God's kingdom, and to do his will. We declare our dependency upon God for all things: provision for temporal necessities, acquittal for sin, and protection from all manner of evil and the evil one. In the closing statement of praise we sound forth that God is the greatest!

To help us appreciate further the *confessional potentiality* of the prayer, we might imagine it recast and amplified as statements of faith.[76] For example:

> We believe God is our heavenly Father, who planned for our redemption and adopted us into his family. He is above us, yet ever near, powerful and personal, great and gracious, majestic and merciful, holy and helpful.

---

[73] J. Harold Ellens. "Communication Theory and Petitionary Prayer," *Journal of Psychology and Theology* Vol. 5, no. 1 (1977): 52.

[74] Ibid.

[75] Ibid., 52 & 53.

[76] These creedal-like statements are based on the interpretations given in this writer's volume on the Lord's Prayer (see notes 56 & 65).

We believe God's name is synonymous with his identity and character, and that we should hold his name in highest regard, never misusing it, for to do so is an act of disrespect.

We believe we enter the kingdom of God's grace by faith as we receive Jesus Christ as our Savior and Lord. We understand that we must surrender daily to the Holy Spirit's leading in order to increase and persevere in the kingdom, and so that we may receive a rich welcome in the kingdom of God's glory.

We believe we are privileged to participate in the doing of God's predestined will for this world, that we have an obligation to be faithful in complying with his prescribed will for all people, and that we should seek to know and do God's will for us as individuals and as communities of faith.

We believe we may approach God for our daily needs because he is concerned for our well-being. He desires that we be provided for so that we may enjoy life to the full, and that we may successfully advance his kingdom and do his will. We acknowledge, however, that we should request only what we need, that we should consider the needs of others, and that we should never forget to thank God for all his benefits.

We believe we are in debt to God because we are sinners, that God offered the death and resurrection of Jesus as payment for our debt, and that we must acknowledge Christ as our personal Savior and Lord in order to be justified to enter God's kingdom. After entering we know we must forgive the sins of others as the condition for God's forgiving our on-going sins.

We believe we need to pray for God's protection on a daily basis because of the many challenges and threats to our Christian living. We know God may test us, and so we ask for leniency. We need to put on the full armor of God in order to guard against giving in to our sinful nature, and in order to do battle successfully against the evils of the world and the attacks of the Evil One.

We believe God will have the ultimate victory, that Jesus Christ will return to gather the elect and defeat the Evil One. We believe that the unseen eternal realm belongs to God, that he is the All-Powerful One, and that he deserves all the glory and praise forever and ever. And it shall be so!

The text of the Lord's Prayer is a container of belief, a compendium of the gospel. Praying it is a means of communicating and confessing the belief contained within it. As reciting creeds and singing hymns are circulating media, so in praying the Lord's Prayer is the faith contained within it circulated, transmitted, shared, and a bond cultivated between all who share in the praying. Praying the prayer is a means of unification and proclamation. The Lord's Prayer has *confessional* value.

There is also *educational* value to the study and praying of the prayer. The great wealth of Christian truth which is compressed into the prayer's phrases has been acknowledged through the centuries by the church. The prayer is an essential source of learning about our faith. Many catechisms have been written for church membership instruction which include the study of the Ten Commandments, the Apostles' Creed, and the Lord's Prayer. We've cited previously Tertullian's label, *compendium of the whole gospel*, Martin Luther's description of the trilogy of the Catechism, a *digest of doctrine*, and Philip Schaff's characterization of the Lord's Prayer as *the gospel in a nutshell*. To examine the prayer's inclusions is to become exposed to this *digest of doctrine*. To pray the prayer is to enable those beliefs to become instilled in believers' minds and hearts. Praying the prayer, therefore, serves as a mnemonic aid for learning its contents.

G. Campbell Morgan's comments on the prayer being an example of an *index prayer* help us appreciate its instructional significance.

> It has been affirmed and correctly so that this is not a new prayer. It's every petition is to be found in the Talmudic writings...There can be little doubt, however, that the men who heard the Master, when He first gave them the prayer, were familiar with all its petitions. In all probability they had used them constantly in their worship from childhood up...[Jesus]

gathered together the things with which they were most familiar and placed them in such perfect relation to each other as to reveal as never before the whole plane of prayer...The Jewish Rabbis taught the people what were known as index prayers. These consisted of a collection of brief sentences, each one of which suggested a subject of prayer. One of their habits of praying was to take such an index prayer, recite one petition at a time, and elaborate it in the presence of God by carrying out its thought, and endeavoring to express its full intent. In that sense the Lord's Prayer also is an index prayer.[77]

The fact also that it is an example of an index prayer tells us that the contents are an index of themes which when prayed provide an outline of the essential themes of Christian belief and devotion. Teaching and praying the prayer, therefore, assists in passing on the faith to the next generation of believers. The content, outline and use of the Lord's Prayer demonstrate its *confessional, educational* and *transmissional* values.

Another educational value of the Lord's Prayer is the one most often voiced, that it is a model for praying, a model which the pattern and outline of the prayer provides. To be sure, the Lord's Prayer is intended to be prayed with other disciples as the Lukan text affirms. However, the words of Jesus prior to the Matthean version, "This, then is how you should pray:...," suggest to us the prayer is also a model for praying. The Lord's Prayer is at one and the same time a prayer to pray and a model prayer. John Stott commented: "According to Matthew he gave it as a pattern to copy (*Pray then like this*), according to Luke as a form to use (11:2, 'When you pray, say...'). We are not obliged to choose, however, for we can both use the prayer as it stands and also model our own praying upon it."[78]

At some point in my immersion in the study of the Lord's Prayer, I decided to discipline myself to pattern my private praying after Jesus' instruction. Daily I begin my private prayers with the following extended prayer which blends acknowledgement of the persons and

---

[77]Morgan, 59.

[78]Stott, 145.

work of the Father, Son and Holy Spirit, with petitions drawn from those of the Lord's Prayer.

> Heavenly Father, thank you for your love and your mercy, your providential care and your plan of salvation, for redeeming us by faith in Christ, and for caring about us all the time. Thank you for your provisions, and I pray for the continuance of them. Thank you for enabling me to be a part of your kingdom and in your service. I pray for your continued help to hallow your name, to increase in your kingdom, to persevere in the faith, and to help others do the same.
>
> Thank you Lord Jesus for being our Savior, our Teacher, Example, and our Friend, for dying on the cross for our sins, for rising from the dead, having victory over Satan and death, and for giving us hope, the promise of our own resurrection. Thank you for your mercy, for opening the way to a right relationship with the Father. I pray for forgiveness of my sins, for a cleansing of my life by the power of your precious blood; and I pray for a filling of your Spirit and love to forgive others.
>
> Thank you Holy Spirit for living within us by faith in Christ, for your power and presence, your comfort and direction. Please strengthen my immediate family [named specifically], our church families, our extended families and our friends. Please abide with us, relieve any of anxiety and direct our ways. Thank you for your leniency regarding our trials. I pray for your continued help and for deliverance from them, for deliverance from my sinful nature, from the evils of the world, and the evil one. Please protect our homes, our vehicles, our work places, our church facilities, our work, our activities and our travels, our bodies, minds, spirits and emotions, all ways; please drive the evil one and his emissaries away in the name and by the power of the blood of Jesus.

This is obviously a very personal example of how the Lord's Prayer may serve as a model both in content and order for private praying.

Certainly we might pray one of the phrases of the Lord's Prayer, and then amplify extemporaneously, as in the rabbinic tradition. In light of these potentialities, we may say the prayer not only has unifying, confessional, educational and transmissional import, it also has *devotional value*.

The Lord's Prayer also possesses *ethical* value. As with the Ten Commandments which may be divided into two sections, four words about devotion to God and six words dealing with appropriate human relations, so also in the Lord's Prayer are given two areas of concern, allegiance to God and duty to others. Max Lucado, in his creative volume mentioned previously, wrote: "In these verses Christ has provided more than a model for prayer, he has provided a model for living."[79] We have the right to pray for protection from evil and the Evil One; we also have the responsibility to live in a manner which guards against influencing others in wrong ways. We have the right to pray for forgiveness of sins; but we also have the responsibility to forgive others. Not only are we given the right to petition God for bread; we are given also the responsibility to help others acquire their bread. We have the right and privilege to enter God's kingdom. We are also given the responsibility to increase in the kingdom and do God's will, and to help others enter and increase and do God's will as well. We have the right to call upon God. We have the responsibility to honor God's name and reputation. We have the privilege of praying the Lord's Prayer together with other Christians. We have the responsibility to so live that we preserve the unity of the Christian witness. These are some of the ethical implications and values of the prayer. Praying it regularly is a reminder of our responsibilities as disciples of Christ.

We may say the Lord's Prayer also has *symbolic* value. As we have stated previously, praying the Lord's Prayer is a *mark of identity* and allegiance. Praying the prayer in the assembly is a group sign to others that we desire to be known as Christian. In another way, it may be fair to say that praying it has become for Christians a kind of sacramental event. We may think of its use as a thing-event through which we are brought into the presence of a holy God and place ourselves in a posi-

---

[79]Lucado, 5.

tion of receiving God's grace. Praying the prayer may be viewed as a door to the sacred.[80] Many times we have difficulty finding the right words to express the inexpressible. Praying the Lord's Prayer helps us in those times when all other words fail. It says more than we could ever say, even when we are not thoroughly cognitive of the significance of each phrase. The prayer says more than it means. It represents and symbolizes something greater and loftier and more profound than our words could ever convey, that is the deepest longings of our hearts.

From the above we see that praying the Lord's Prayer in corporate worship especially, as well as in private devotions, has many values and potentialities. Praying together cultivates unity as the Body of Christ and enhances communion with God. As a kingdom of priests to the world, we have the obligation to band together and become mature ambassadors (Jn. 17:20-23, Eph. 4:13). Praying the Lord's Prayer together assists in nurturing the sense of oneness and togetherness we have by faith in Christ. This is a unity evermore needed in a world which seems bent on promoting values which only lead to the fracturing of families and the stifling of the discussion of religious values in public discourse. We must do all we can as Christians to foster wholeness, unity, harmony, and spiritual maturity. The study and intentional and sensible use of the Lord's Prayer in worship in particular is one ingredient in God's program for cultivating these qualities.

---

[80]John Macquarrie. *A Guide to the Sacraments* (New York: Continuum, 1997), 14.

Chapter Seven
Preaching with a Manuscript

Although the emphasis of this volume is on the biblical bases for the ordering and inclusions of public worship and the Brethren tradition of the rites and ceremonies of the church, praying, preaching and offering musical inclusions have an intimate and regular place in weekly public worship. Corporate worship is the context within which they serve. Therefore, a chapter on each has been included, with the present one giving attention to the values of manuscript preaching.[81]

It could be said that there are as many styles or methods of preaching as there are preachers. Each pastor has a unique personality with a voice all his own, a particular temperament, body presence, and facial gestures. However, there are three major approaches for preaching. Some preachers speak *extemporaneously*. That is, they may prepare ahead of time, perhaps develop an outline of major points to make; yet when they deliver their sermons, they "make up," if you will, the text for the message as they speak before a congregation. Other preachers, perhaps the largest group, prepare and develop a substantial *outline* of the points and sub-points to present then deliver their sermons with *notes*, making those points and "filling in the blanks" with on-the-spot connective comments, elaborations, and illustrations.

The third major historic tradition, what we might refer to as a *classic* approach, is the *manuscript method*. Preachers who preach from a manuscript prepare very thoroughly, spending healthy portions of time fashioning their sermons with the best language and formulation of thought of which they are capable. In New England and other locations for much of our national history, this method was the standard procedure for many preachers in preparation and delivery. It is my view that this method remains a superior approach for the production of the

---

[81]This is a revised version of Peter E. Roussakis, "Why I Believe in Preaching with a Manuscript," *Preaching*, The Professional Journal for Preachers, Vol. 16, No. 4, January-February 2001, 34-35. Used with permission.

best sermon content and for the long-lasting spiritual growth of parishioners. Accepting the fact that it may not be the most natural approach for other pastors, who may be very fine preachers in their own right and who use a different method, it has been for me during much of my career in preaching, and that of many of my colleagues, the method which is most appropriate for our presentation of the Gospel and through which we find the finest opportunity to develop and communicate God's Word to a world that needs more than milk. We need the *meat* of the Scriptures. A few of my Brethren clergy colleagues prepare a manuscript of their sermon for each week, and then reduce it to an outline for delivery, needless to say, with significant private rehearsal. Either way, delivering from a manuscript or an outline of it, I believe it is worthy of prospective and experienced pastors to consider stepping up the quality of their preparation for the weekly sermon through the discipline of well-formulated and well-crafted manuscripts. The following are some of the values and benefits of doing so.

Preparing a manuscript forces the preacher to spend sufficient, intentional time in study, thinking about the meaning and message of a particular passage, analyzing the biblical material, formulating and preparing articulation of the major themes to be presented. What usually results is a *more well-crafted and thoughtful presentation* of God's Word than might otherwise be offered. Whereas with extemporaneous preaching or preaching with notes one might argue there is afforded greater eye-to-eye contact between preacher and congregation, such attention does not ensure that the sermon will embody substantive material. Moreover, it does not follow that manuscript preachers do not have sufficient eye-to-eye contact. Skillful manuscript preachers will learn how to present themselves and look at the text when they need to and when they do not to provide for a very pleasing delivery which keeps parishioners' attention. Preachers in congregations with greater budgets for advanced technology may even indulge themselves in acquiring a teleprompter. If a sermon is interesting, well crafted and pleasingly delivered, parishioners will be engaged and naturally maintain their focus.

When preachers provide well-prepared and articulated sermons, there is a greater potential, it seems to me, for parishioners to receive a worthwhile body of persuasion and instruction. The persons in the pews will benefit more in the long run, their body of engaged biblical material enlarged and deepened when being exposed to a manuscript prepared sermon. In other words, with this format and approach, *greater learning* may take place; there is a greater growth potential fostered. Why is this so?

One of the reasons why growth may be greater is because of the power of the *variety of word usages* which pre-thought affords. So often it may be observed that preachers who deliver sermons extemporaneously or with limited outline notes will utilize the same terminology over and over simply because the on-the-spot vocabulary of most of us in American society today is not as broad as that of those in former periods or of those who are educated in the British tradition where reading requirements and habits are more extensive. Of necessity for many, this writer/preacher included, pre-thought and articulation is needed to provide as varied an array of word usages as possible to provide many word concepts to define, describe and illustrate the sometimes unfamiliar and theologically mature themes of Christianity. Needless to say, hearing the same language over and over is not as interesting as a well-crafted and descriptive body of language. In other words, communication will be more effective, the experience of listening to sermons will be more interesting, and therefore, the learning potential will be greater.

Another value of writing sermons is that the material presented may be *preserved in print* and distributed to parishioners subsequently for their further consideration, digestion, and reinforcement. My experience has been that parishioners develop an eagerness for Scripture study when they know they will be receiving the pamphlet-size productions of my sermons. They value collecting and reading them for through-the-week continued study and personal edification. A hunger for God's Word is cultivated.

It is very useful as well for preachers to prepare their sermons in writing because they produce a *body of theological formulation* which enables them to evaluate which aspects of the Christian corpus they have covered in their preaching and teaching and which themes and passages or books of the Bible they have neglected. The experience of writing sermons thus aids in the planning process for future sermon development.

Similarly, by submitting to the discipline of writing sermon manuscripts, pastors soon realize they are producing a body of theological insight which reveals their theological orientation and positions. At some point in one of the churches I served I decided that the congregation and I would both benefit from my preparing and delivering a series of sermons dealing with the major categories of Christian belief. Because I was intentional about this task, with the additional foresight that the preserved material might be useful as literature for church membership classes, I was very careful to articulate in language which was not only faithful to the Scriptures, but also accessible to learners, written with as fine a quality as I could provide. The result was that the people grew immeasurably as they heard the messages on Sundays, received in short order the printed copies, then eventually were able to consult the whole collection in a bound format. Furthermore, I received the satisfaction of having formulated my theological position statements. *I wrote my theology of the Christian faith*, and, as years passed when persons would ask me where I stood on this or that issue or concept, I was better prepared to respond because I had taken the time to think about many subjects, and in the course of studying and articulating, developed statements and descriptions which otherwise may not have come into light. The experience revealed and developed my theological orientation. I had a better understanding of where I stood theologically, and so did others.

By writing and producing sermons in print the *instructional influence and ministry* can be extended to a wider audience as the sermons may be passed to others, one-on-one to inquirers, in classes, through the mail to seekers and potential worshipers, to friends, and to those for whom we pray will take faith matters more seriously and come to faith in Christ. The potential for extended witness is created when sermons are in print.

Taped sermons are very valuable tools for ministry to others, particularly those with sight difficulties and those confined to their homes or nursing care facilities. For those not experiencing such challenges, having printed sermons enables them to *locate fairly quickly key ideas* they wish to remember by simply marking the location of the items in question. The material may be referred to over and over again as desired.

I have found that a greater bond of love and appreciation is developed between pastor and parishioners and that they are more focused on the application of God's Word in their lives when they possess and may refer to the *collection of sermons* produced. They have the pastor's instruction with them in their homes. It helps cultivate a more total life-style awareness of their obligation to take seriously the teachings of the Scriptures and to apply them to their everyday circumstances. In times of despondency parishioners may refer to sermons which focus attention on God's care, their need to persevere, how they can cope, and so forth.

Additionally pastors will develop the satisfaction and assurance that their ministries of the Word will have *lasting effect*. Even when they may move on to other venues of service, their articulations will remain with the people and be a continued source of learning and encouragement. Preachers will have a legacy they will have deposited with those under their care.

Printed sermons may also be of *benefit to Sunday School and small group teachers and leaders* in support of their Christian education efforts. The sermons may become a part of the body of literature on a particular subject for a class.

Pastorally speaking, a sermon manuscript may be very helpful for the preacher to *guard against saying things off-the-cuff* which, without forethought, may be unintentionally hurtful to someone in the congregation. It is too easy for pastors to put their feet in their mouths, so to speak, when they have not taken the time to think about the possible consequences or implications of their words.

Finally, our appreciation for manuscript sermons should be heightened when we realize the great inspiration and instruction we receive by reading the preserved sermons of John Calvin, Martin Luther, John Wesley (1703-1791), George Whitefield (1714-1770), the Puritans, Jonathan Edwards (1703-1758), and so many others of the past and present. When we realize the great influence these preachers had in peoples' lives in their own day, and of the countless others through the years, we come to the conclusion that writing and preserving sermons has great value and ministry potential. Moreover, in an era, such as ours, when the forces of evil seem to be rising up in acute fashion, we need more than ever, to deepen the faith of parishioners and all others who will give a listening ear to the principles, practices and hope which are given in the Holy Scriptures. Disseminating those truths through written and printed media is one way of edifying the families of faith.

Chapter Eight
Music in Worship

Music is a part of our lives. If we are not professional or amateur musicians we still listen to music when we turn on the radio or watch television, when we go to the grocery store or the mall. Music is all around us. It is an integral part of our culture. It's a part of life. Why is this so? Suzanne K. Langer (1895-1985), former professor of philosophy at Radcliff, Columbia University, and Connecticut College for Women, described this relationship between music and daily life. "The tonal structures we call music bear a close logical similarity to the forms of human feeling, forms of growth and of attenuation, flowing and stowing, conflict and resolution, speed, arrest, terrific excitement, calm or subtle activation and dreamy lapses, not joy or sorrow perhaps, but the poignancy of either or both, the greatness and brevity and eternal passing of everything virtually felt...Music is a tonal analogue of emotive life...Music has import, and this import is the pattern of sentience, the pattern of life itself, as it is felt and directly known."[82]

The capacity of music to mirror the rhythms of our emotions makes it a natural for playing a prominent role in society. From the beginning of human history people have danced and sung and played something. The ancient Hebrews, our ancestors in the faith, were no exception. Through their tradition we realize that music was ordained by God to be a part of, enhance, and serve as a vehicle for worshiping God. It is important, therefore, that we think about the significance of music in worship. We shall speak first about this in overall categories, then direct our attention to the contributions of vocal music in general, choral music in particular, and conclude with a discussion of instrumental music.[83]

---

[82]Suzanne K. Langer, *Feeling and Form* (New York: Charles Scribner's Sons, 1952), 27-29.

[83]This chapter is a revision of Peter E. Roussakis, "Music in Christian Worship," *FOUNDATION 2000: Faculty Essays for Ministry Professionals* (Donaldson, IN: Graduate Theological Foundation, 2000). Used with permission.

Significance of Music in Worship

Praising God. The first purpose of music in worship is to enable people to praise God, to give thanks for all God has done and is doing on our behalf. With so many references, perhaps as many as seven hundred regarding music in the Bible, and a whole book of Psalms intended to be sung, we get the point. "Come, let us sing for joy to the Lord...and exalt him with music and song" (Ps. 95:1-2). Music is intended by God to be a vehicle for all people to give thanks and praise. This is the first duty of the creature to the Creator and it is natural that music should be used for that purpose. In his classic text on music in worship, Joseph N. Ashton (1868-1946), former professor of music history at Brown University, wrote: "It is not by mere accident that music has always been used in religious worship, for religion and music arise from the same general part of our being. Religion is the most intimate of all human experiences, and music is the most intimate of the arts. Music is at once the most subjective and the least concrete of all the arts; its subjective-ness is the most personal, its substance the least tangible. It has the valuable property of stimulating the emotions and strengthening consciousness, yet at the same time regulating them through the sense of balance and proportion inherent in the art of music itself. Music is the ideal art for religious worship."[84]

The relationship of music with worship is so significant that Martin Luther said: "We are able to adduce only this one point at present, namely, that experience proves that, next to the Word of God, only music deserves being extolled as the mistress and governess of the feelings of the human heart...the Fathers and Prophets desired not in vain that nothing be more intimately linked up with the Word of God than music."[85]

From accounts in 1 Chronicles we learn that it was under King David's leadership that worship music became organized. Large numbers of Levites, with no less than 288 skilled leaders, were trained to

---

[84]Joseph N. Ashton, *Music in Worship: The Use of Music in the Church Service* New Introduction by Peter E. Roussakis (Bristol, Indiana: Wyndham Hall Press, 2001) [First published by Pilgrim Press, Boston, 1943], 8.

[85]Walter E. Buszin, "Luther on Music," *The Musical Quarterly*, Vol. 22 (1946), 81.

lead as singers and instrumentalists. This practice continued under Solomon when the Temple was built and during the revivals under Hezekiah and Josiah to provide for the praise of God in worship. "Ascribe to the Lord the glory due his name; worship the Lord with the splendor of his holiness" (Ps. 29:2). One of the purposes of music is to mirror that splendor.

Proclaiming the Revelation of God. The second significant purpose of music in worship is to enable people to proclaim the revelation of God, to communicate the message God has entrusted to us as preserved in the Holy Scriptures of the Bible. In the Old Testament we read that David "set apart" some of the sons of Asaph, Heman and Jeduthun, the three primary music directors, "for the ministry of prophesying, accompanied by harps, lyres and cymbals" (1 Chr. 25:1; see also 1 Chr. 6:31-47). Prophesying in this context did not mean predicting. These persons forth-told the revelation of God to the people by singing the message to the accompaniment of a musical instrument. These were like traveling minstrels, like the folk singers of the 1960's who sang songs of social import accompanied on the guitar. The musicians served as proclaimers of God's truth, often warning the people that unfaithfulness, neglecting worship, or worshiping false gods would lead to severe consequences. Their simple song form was probably similar to our hymns. With repeated music for each stanza, hymns enable people today to execute the relatively simple musical tasks of praising and proclaiming, to be a part of the worshiping experience.

As the musicians under David communicated God's word, so all who are modestly musically gifted by God have the privilege of forth-telling the stories of redemption, proclaiming in song the attributes of God, and giving witness to the experience of God in our lives by faith in Jesus Christ. It's not only the choir or other vocal group which sings the tenets of the faith. All worshipers are given a role in the communication (e.g. Ps. 145:10, 150:6). Many hymns are metrical paraphrases of scripture, such as Isaac Watt's rendering of Psalm 90, "Our God, Our Help in Ages Past." Many other hymns are flooded with allusions to scripture, as are the hymns of Charles Wesley (1707-1788). Still others are interpretations of Christian experience, as so many so-called gospel hymns illustrate. Hymns, therefore, may be viewed as containers of Christian belief. As S. T. Kimbrough remarked, "the hymns of the church are theology."[86] S. Paul Schilling described hymns as "embodiments of Christian belief."[87] John Wesley regarded hymns as "doctrinal manifestoes."[88] Singing worshipers, therefore, are proclaimers of those hymnicly conceived expressions of belief.

Strengthening the Church. A third significance of music in worship is that through the experience of offering praise to God and proclaiming God's revelation the church is strengthened, edified, built up in the faith. The church becomes strengthened as those gifted in music exercise their gift. Paul wrote: "Just as each of us has one body with many members, and these members do not all have the same function, so in Christ we who are many form one body, and each member belongs to all of the others. We have different gifts, according to the grace given us" (Rom. 12:4-6a.). "When you come together, everyone has a hymn, or a word of instruction, a revelation, a tongue or an interpretation. All these must be done for the strengthening of the church" (1 Cor. 14:26). Through the exercise of their musical talent, musicians gain a sense of fulfillment and listeners are blessed by the musical offerings, not only because the music may be inspiring, but also because they are moved by the fact that their fellow Christians are serving in that way. In addition, as the whole group sings hymns and other types of songs, a sense of communal identity and spirit is fostered; as the hymn says: "We are one in the Spirit." Music enables that oneness to be cultivated. Karl Barth (1886-1968) took this idea a step further by identifying musical expression as an essential ingredient of a Christian community. "The praise of God which constitutes the community and its assemblies seeks to bind and commit and therefore to be expressed, to well up and be sung in concert. The Christian community sings. It is

---

[86]S. T. Kimbrough, Jr. "Hymns Are Theology," *Theology Today*, XLII, No. 1 (April 1985), 59.

[87]S. Paul Schilling, *The Faith We Sing: How the Message of Hymns Can Enhance Christian Belief* (Philadelphia: The Westminster Press, 1983), 23.

[88]Ernest J. Rattenbury, *The Evangelical Doctrines of Charles Wesley's Hymns* London: The Epworth Press, 1941), 62.

not a choral society. Its singing is not a concert. But from inner, material necessity it sings. Singing is the highest form of human expression. What we can say and must say quite confidently is that the community which does not sing is not the community."[89]

Cultivating Christian Character. The fourth significant point about music in worship is that music helps cultivate Christian character. Yes, music is intimately connected with spiritual character development. Its use can either facilitate healthy character development, or accentuate and promote ungodly ideas and patterns of behavior. The apostle Paul encouraged Christians to make a connection between their position under Christ and their behavior. He told them at length to rid their minds and conduct of all that is impure, to put on the new self, to clothe themselves with Christ-like virtues. Within that context he wrote: "Let the word of Christ dwell in you richly as you teach and admonish one another with all wisdom, and as you sing psalms, hymns and spiritual songs with gratitude in your hearts to God" (Col. 3:16). Through the singing of sacred songs, therefore, the truths of God abide in the heart and mind, impressing and instilling Christ-like thoughts and inclinations. As early as classical antiquity philosophers spoke out regarding the relationship between music and character. Aristotle, for example, held that music affects character and the soul.[90] If worship music can assist people to develop Christ-like virtues, then it becomes the committed Christian's responsibility to avoid music which fosters spiritually unhealthy thoughts and attributes. It becomes the church music director's obligation to choose music which cultivates Godly sensibilities.

Someone may ask: "How can music affect us in these ways? How does music assist in instilling ideas into our minds?" The answers are not as mysterious as they may seem. As an art form music speaks to the total person, the senses as well as the intellect. "I will sing with the spirit, and I will sing with the mind also" (1 Cor. 14:15). Music relates to

---

[89]Karl Barth, *Church Dogmatics*, Vol. 4.3 (Edinburgh: T. & T. Clark, 1962), 866-867.

[90]Aristotle, *Politics* Book VIII (1340) (New York: Penguin Books edition, 1981), 464-467.

us and mirrors the emotive rhythms of our lives through the variety of ways the ingredients of music are fashioned and performed in each piece. Music consists of *sounds* which can be higher or lower in pitch, longer or shorter in duration, louder or softer in dynamics. Tones can be grouped in pulses of three counts, four counts, or any other grouping a composer chooses for the pulse or beat of a piece, otherwise known as *meter*. Melodies and harmonies have a *rhythm* (the combination of the long and short durations of pitches) of their own which shapes the musical ideas expressed. All of the above may be rendered in a faster or slower speed, or *tempo*. When combined with words, the ingredients of music serve to enliven, heighten and interpret, or capture the sense and mood of the words. In these ways music's ingredients serve to impress the revelation of God on and in the minds and hearts of those who hear and sing.

It is very important what music we listen to or perform because of the inherent capacity of music to affect our inner selves. Likewise, it is important for us to realize the influence of worship music, particularly congregational singing, upon the lives of all who worship. It is very understandable, therefore, why John Calvin viewed music as a "funnel" which directs the word of God into the heart of the believer.[91] As we know from Paul: "Faith comes from hearing the message, and the message is heard through the word of Christ" (Rom. 10:17). Thus the importance of music in the hearing process.

Most people are moved spiritually when they can sing or hear well-chosen and performed choral and instrumental music in worship. More than ever music plays an important and integral role in the worship life of the church. Thanks be to God for this special gift through which we may praise and proclaim the revelation of God by which the church is strengthened, and which can help cultivate an inclination toward Godly virtues.

---

[91] Calvin used this imagery in his Preface to the *Genevan Psalter* of 1542, translated and discussed by Charles Garside, Jr. in "Calvin's Preface to the Psalter: A Re-Appraisal," *The Musical Quarterly* Vol. 37 (October 1951), 571.

Vocal Music

As mentioned above, in the Bible there are many references to music, particularly in the Old Testament. In the New Testament we read of the occasion of the Last Supper when Jesus and the disciples sang a hymn before departing for the evening. In two Pauline passages the apostle mentions the use of psalms, hymns and songs in the community of faith (Eph. 5:19, Col. 3:16). The *psalms* probably refer to the accepted 150 psalms of the Old Testament. *Hymns* were probably well-accepted and more recently composed songs of the early Christian community and, presumably, sung without any accompaniment. *Spiritual songs* most likely referred to extemporaneous singing by individuals led by the Spirit of God in worship or in informal settings. As we examine such references we can identify two important functions of vocal music in worship.

Faith Expression. The more obvious use of vocal music was and is as a means of faith expression. From the Psalms we read: "Shout for joy to the Lord all the earth. Worship the Lord with gladness; come before him with joyful songs" (Psalm 100:1). "Praise the Lord. Sing to the Lord a new song, his praise in the assembly of the saints" (Ps. 149:1). "Praise the Lord; praise God in his sanctuary" (Ps. 150:1). To sing to God or about God is a natural human response of God's children. We express our faith in worship through the spoken and sung word. Some of what we sing is praise-oriented. Many hymns and songs, vocal solos and anthems are prayer expressions. Others challenge us to commitment. All are vehicles of *faith expression*.

In classic worship in particular, the choir or a soloist may introduce the service with some kind of musical sentence called the introit. All the people declare their faith through the singing of the *Gloria Patri* and the *Doxology*; both are doxological, as they are short vocal affirmations of glory (Gk. *doxa*) to God. Hymns, anthems and solos are containers and communicators of faith. Each has text which directs our minds and emotions God-ward. Congregations, choirs and soloists, therefore, have a prophetic role in worship. Together they forth-tell the timeless themes of the faith, thoughts and feelings of people of faith. The tunes serve to enliven the texts, aurally expressing and interpreting the emotive dimensions of the texts, providing a powerful mode of transmitting the messages, serving as means of proclaiming, praising, declaring, professing and thanking. Vocal music helps punctuate significant ideas, placing emphasis on particular themes and emotions which mere speech cannot do in the same way. With sound our spirits are stirred even more. What a gift God has given us to express faith: our voices, no matter what the level of natural singing ability.

Faith Formation and Preservation. As explained above, the singing of psalms, hymns and songs is one way the truths of the faith become instilled, embedded in the hearts and minds of believers. The information about Christ becomes internalized and takes hold.. We have understood for many years that people learn most effectively by doing. Through participation, that which we do becomes a part of us. Effort, thought and feeling all play a part in the process of musical expression and impression. Sacred song, with its participatory and sound dimensions, facilitates the instillation of the sacred word. It assists, therefore, in the process of *faith formation.*

Moreover, through singing sacred songs we play a part in *preserving the faith* we wish to pass on to the next generation. Some musical styles may come and go; but the regular, steady, thoughtful singing of hymns, anthems and service music, helps perpetuate the worship of God and the message of Jesus Christ to which we have been called to relate each week in worship. When we sing a hymn about the cross, for example, we journey back to the crucifixion through our imaginations. We cannot retrieve the event as it happened. What we retrieve is an image, a conceptualization and an interpretation of it, and we bring it into our present. This is faith forming, faith preserving.[92] Vocal music has the unique capacity to help us make associations and to conceptualize what such experiences may have been like, and thereby transfer an impression of the foundations of our faith from the past into the present. This is *faith formation and preservation.* Certainly when selecting texts of anthems, hymns and solos, it is necessary to pay attention to the theol-

---

[92]This concept of faith formation and preservation is drawn in part from the thought of Linda J. Clark, given in her *Music in Churches* (Bethseda, Maryland: Alban Institute, 1994).

ogy they embody and would potentially be instilled. Because of the power music has in conveying belief and impressing faith, each piece should be evaluated for its literary quality and doctrinal suitability.

In sum, when choirs and soloists sing, and when congregations sing hymns, other songs and doxologies, they are engaged in one of the most significant and pleasant worship acts. Through the singing of sacred songs we express faith; we tell it musically; and through the telling of it, faith is being formed, preserved, enriched, enhanced, and passed on. From these understandings we can appreciate more than ever why "Brethren worship has always given a major place to congregational singing."[93] Can you imagine worship without vocal music? Through it we glorify God and strengthen the church of Jesus Christ, in whose name we sing.

Choral Singing

Choirs and other vocal groups have a specialized function in worship. The use of choral singing in worship is God-intended. The basic function of the choir in the Old Testament era was to give musical praise to God. "Let everything that has breath praise the Lord" (Ps. 150:6). Both singers and instrumentalists were chosen (1 Chr. 15:1-2), gave all or such part of their time as necessary (1 Chr. 9:33; 16:37), were educated and trained (1 Chr. 15:22; 25:7), were consecrated (Num. 8:5-14), wore robes (1 Chr. 15:27), and it is believed were provided housing (Num. 7:73) as is the case today for cathedral musicians in England (see also 1 Chr. 15:14-28; 25:1-31; 2 Chr. 30:21; Num. 7:67 and 12:45-46 where both men and women sang in choirs). Biblical example demonstrates the special place choirs held in the life of the worshiping community. Corporate worship as it has developed, however, contains more than the element of praise. It is for this reason that we can discern several roles the choir plays in today's worship.

Pastoral Role. The choir is part of the liturgical personnel, part of the worship leadership team. Along with the pastor, instrumentalists, acolytes (candle-lighters) and lectors (readers), the choir provides leadership for worship. Because of their typical visibility and placement in

---

[93] *The Brethren Encyclopedia* Volume 2, 1378.

most congregations, choir members help lead the congregation in the recitation of responsive readings and unison prayers. In musical ways the choir provides support for congregational singing. If a new tune is used in a particular service, the choir may demonstrate the appropriate rendering of it. In both musical and non-musical ways we may say the choir ministers to the congregation in worship through its leadership functions. The choir has a pastoral role.

In addition, participation in choir is a pastoral ministry to its members as it gives them an avenue of service and the opportunity to develop their interests and abilities in music. Choir also has recreational and therapeutic values for its members. There's nothing like a good sing to lift one's spirit. For most persons, participation in choir is fun. The pleasure of music-making is a strong incentive for many to sing as a point of entry into church life. It may be viewed, therefore, as a vehicle of outreach as well.

Priestly Role. Part of the choir's function in classic worship may be said to be priestly as the choir sings portions of the liturgy such as various forms of service music (introits, responses, sung prayers, choral benedictions). Upon occasion the choir may sing an appropriate anthem or motet as a prayer of confession or other element of the worship order. Also, the choir helps to keep the service elements moving, so to speak, by providing aural-thought connectors in the form of responses, enhancing the prayers of the clergy and the people, singing in a way on behalf of the congregation. The choir helps to announce worship through the introit or a choral call to worship and to dismiss the people with a choral benediction or benediction response. In these ways choirs have a priestly function.

Prophetic Role. For most choirs the primary effort each week is the rehearsing of anthems which musically support and interpret the biblical theme of the sermon. Usually placed near the sermon, the choir's anthem falls within the proclamation section of the worship service. Through the singing of anthems the choir forth-tells the truths of the Christian faith, musically rendering portions and interpretations of scripture, announcing the Good News to those present. Based on Colossians 3:16 we can say the choir serves to present and impress

God's word in our hearts and minds as it is sung.

Another way to describe the prophetic role of the choir is to say it serves as a bearer of salvation history, both the salvation history of the group which testifies to God's goodness and love, and that of the historical record, the Hebrew and Christian scriptures. Since anthems have words, they are primarily concerned with the narrative of the Christian story and the faith-interpretation of the scriptural accounts. Along with the pastor and lector, therefore, the choir has the unique role of bringing before the people the message of God's activity in human life. The choir in its prophetic role interprets the word of God to, and offers praise, contrition and petition on behalf of the congregation.

Performance Role. When asked what is their philosophy of sacred music, many choir directors and organists say they strive to perform the best possible and appropriate music in the best possible way. While this idea is a good one, it is somewhat narrow. It lacks an understanding of the other dimensions of sacred music given above. When encouraged to speak further on the subject, such musicians might admit that by best they mean musical-theoretical integrity of the highest order in composition, selection and performance. Again, this is a good view. However, when taken alone, good performance from musical standards is not the only goal of sacred music and certainly does not ensure that the performance will have either suitability in worship or that the people will be spiritually tuned in to the thoughts of the texts.

Having said that, we must say that choirs do perform; and the music they perform adds beauty to a service of worship, whether that beauty be an aural-atmosphere mood of solemnity, longing, rejoicing, or any other emotion. The choir and instrumentalists have dominant roles to play in enhancing worship through musical mood. Certainly the scriptures tell the story of people who have experienced the ups and downs of life, of confessing and forgiving, of anger and tension and love, and the like. The choir ministers to the congregation as it recreates these emotions through effective performance. This is important because the emotions are a significant channel for the communication and instillation of God's truths. The combination of apprehension through the senses and comprehension through the mind is a powerful one. Music plays a vital role in the process of communication.

As creatures of the Creator we need to be good stewards of God's gift of music. Choirs will honor God by spending their time well in rehearsal and striving for the finest and most effective rendering of the works they sing. Performing skillfully is a biblical admonition (Ps. 33:3) and is good stewardship. Moreover, as performers, choir members have the opportunity to be exposed to and develop an appreciation for fine sacred choral literature. They will learn as they help the congregation grow aesthetically. In addition, through effective rehearsal and performance the choir has the opportunity to learn proper vocal and choral techniques which can cultivate a great sense of personal fulfillment, foster stewardship of abilities, and help render the music they sing more effectively. The more effective the performance, the greater the chance of inspiring and instructing the congregation. In these ways choir experience functions pastorally to itself and to the congregation through performance.

What a privilege it is for choirs to be able to enrich the worship of God as they intone the truths and emotions of the Christian faith; as they lead congregations through the support of congregational singing and the singing of service music; and as they perform music to lift hearts and minds God-ward. Pastoral, priestly, prophetic and performance aspects of choir service make it one of the most enjoyable, meaningful, rewarding and important ministries of Christ's church.

Having considered the ministry of text-based music, we shall now discuss the values and roles of non-verbal music in the worshiping church.

Instrumental Music

As we know, sounds can make us feel joyful; they can aurally mirror feelings, move us to tears of inspiration and gratitude. Sounds are powerful "things." God intended for worshipers to use sounds in worship. Emphasis is given in Psalm 150 on how God can be praised in worship through the sounds of trumpets, harp and lyre, tambourine, strings, flute, and cymbals; with everything that has breath to sound forth.

God is to be praised with brass, wind, string and percussion instruments; and, according to Psalm 150, with sacred dance and human voice. In Psalm 150 we have the most complete list of musical instruments found in any one place in the Bible. The list is certainly not exhaustive, however. Other instruments are mentioned elsewhere; and, of course, through the years new instruments have been invented and are used today.

Biblical Precedent. In 1 Chronicles 15 and 16 is recorded the occasion of David bringing to Jerusalem the Ark of the Covenant, the container in which was kept the tablets of the Ten Commandments. The Ark was placed in the Israelites' portable worship center, the Tent of Meeting (Tabernacle). David appointed some of the Levites to minister through instrumental music. Asaph, a cymbal player, was appointed the chief musician who led the other instrumentalists and singers in the musical praise of God (1 Chr. 16:4-7).

Under the reign of Solomon the Temple was built. At the first worship service, discussed in 2 Chronicles 5, the Ark was brought into the inner sanctuary of the Temple. All the musicians "stood on the east side of the altar, dressed in fine linen and playing cymbals, harps and lyres. They were accompanied by 120 priests sounding trumpets. The trumpeters and singers joined in unison, as with one voice, to give praise and thanks to the Lord. Accompanied by trumpets, cymbals and other instruments, they raised their voices in praise to the Lord and sang" (2 Chr. 5:12-13).

In the New Testament there is a strange silence regarding instrumental music. We may understand this, however, because at that time the church was in its infancy. Many gathered and worshiped in homes; and, with the destruction of the Temple, Jews who became Christians probably would not have thought to utilize instruments in a non-sanctuary worship setting. They did sing psalms, however (Col. 3:16, Eph. 4:19), which by definition of the term implies singing to the accompaniment of a musical instrument.

Roles of Instrumental Music. From the above examples we discern two main roles of instrumental music in worship. First, instruments help create an aural atmosphere for the worshiping experience. They help in conceptualizing the splendor of the glory due to God in worship (Ps. 29:2). Music by organ, piano, bells, chimes, brass, winds, strings and percussion instruments help set a number of moods appropriate for the various elements of the worship service. Worshipers will gain more from their time together by "taking in," as it were, all that is offered musically. Just because one does not hear words sung along with instrumental music does not mean it is without significance or does not merit worshipers' attention, for instrumental music may be able to capture through sound symbols our longings which are indescribable.

For many of us who attend worship, the first sound we hear when entering the sanctuary is the live or recorded instrumental prelude/gathering music. There is significance to that time. The instrumental sound is present to help parishioners step aside from the routine and trials of the world, to enter into a place set apart from the rest of life to commune with God, to offer adoration, to confess sins, to hear the truths of the faith proclaimed, give thanks, and offer themselves anew to the presence and direction of God in their lives. It is a worthy beginning to a worshiping event. Whether or not worshipers recognize the importance of the prelude or other instrumental service music (e.g. the offertory or the postlude/dismissal music), listen to it, and allow the music to accomplish what it is there to do, is a matter of choice or perhaps local education and tradition. Persons who are inclined to speak during service music, however, should refrain from doing so, out of respect for those who wish to be ministered to by it, and by way of thanksgiving and respect for the ones who are offering the music for the glory of God and the edification of the Body of Christ. Generally understood, the pre-service music is offered as a time for parishioners to prepare their hearts and minds for worship. Allowing themselves to say quiet prayers, or simply to be there as the sounds penetrate our inner selves, can be one of the most therapeutic and respectful things a worshiper can do, respectful to God, to others in attendance, and to the ones playing. On the other hand, especially in many Brethren churches, gathering music is a time when gathering is enjoyed, fellowship is renewed. Pastors and musicians should be flex-

Music in Worship

ible in their appreciation for what is intended or being accomplished during pre-service music.

The second primary role of instrumental music in worship is to support, enhance and enrich solo, congregational and choral singing. The instruments provide musical support and foundation to vocal music and serve to lead singers who might otherwise feel reticent to participate. The instruments, through the choices of combinations of sounds, the loudness or softness of the performance, and the speed at which the music is played, serve to enliven, interpret and "carry along" the singing of the people. To repeat, the instruments assist in the process of impressing the truths of the faith in the minds and hearts of the worshipers, giving them added support for their expressions of worship through hymns and songs, anthems, solos, doxologies and choral sentences.

We may conclude that God intended for the people of faith to use musical instruments in worship. The Bible makes its clear that all types of instruments are acceptable and appropriate when used tastefully, intelligently and skillfully. Instrumental musicians are people who serve God through worship leadership. A sense of fulfillment is cultivated within musicians who feel they have made a contribution to the life of the church.

Instruments produce sounds which musically announce, accompany, enhance and amplify worship singing, aurally conceptualizing attitudes toward and attributes of God, faith, and the worship elements. The sounds carry messages and convey non-verbal meanings, those ideas and feelings which are difficult to express in words.

The moods which instrumental music produce enable worshipers to be transported for a few moments in time from the earthly to the divine realm, filling them with the spiritual, surrounding and infusing them aurally with a sense of the sacred, enabling them to worship, helping to strengthen them for the return to the everyday. All music, vocal and instrumental, is not offered to entertain. It is not included for diversion, just to make people feel good (although it is certainly desired that it would). Music is part of the total worship we offer in gratitude for all God's benefits.

CLASSIC WORSHIP

A Word for Today

We've stated the glory of God is one of the primary aims of Christian worship and should influence what we do and how we do it in the gathered assembly (e.g. Ps. 29:1-2). The co-purpose of corporate worship is the edification of the Body of Christ (e.g. 1 Cor. 14:26). Both purposes should be kept in mind when planning worship, preparing sermons and selecting music. To plan and conduct worship and music which emphasizes one aim to the exclusion of the other produces worship experiences which lack sufficient biblical grounding and which do not minister to all of the family of faith. Planning well and utilizing biblically-informed orders of worship are essential. God was very intentional in his planning and creating and redeeming. We should be intentional and thorough is our planning and conduct of worship as well. The principle which the apostle Paul expressed to the Corinthians regarding the Lord's Supper remembrance is applicable for worship and music planning, rehearsing and conduct as well: "everything should be done in a fitting and orderly way" (1 Cor. 15:40).

At the same time, regarding music in particular, God has enabled us to develop a variety of musical genres and styles with which to offer praise and the other elements of worship. The shapes of some of these modes of musical expression have changed somewhat over time and others have been added. While some traditionalists would like to dismiss some of what exists today in the name of contemporary Christian music, the idea of variety has solid scriptural support (e.g. the psalms, hymns and songs of Col. 3:16). However equivalent those genres may be thought of today, the principle remains. A variety of forms serve to minister to and through the whole Christian community.

In light of the widespread usage of the *praise and worship* genre of congregational singing, and because there exists a distinct polarization within many congregations because of its usage, two cautions must be offered. Whatever styles may be used and combined, they should never be used in such a way as to reduce worship to entertainment, or as a vehicle for personal display (that goes not only for the more contemporary forms, but also for the more classical). We should be in the ministry of cultivating servants, not stars. Whatever styles and media are employed, vocal, choral and instrumental offerings should be thoughtfully selected, rehearsed and performed, for this is God-honoring (e.g. Ps. 33:3).

In addition, churches should not abandon the use of traditional forms of musical expression for they offer in most cases a wider spectrum of Christian themes so appropriate and needed in worship coordination and for the enhancement of spiritual maturation. We must remind ourselves of the co-purposes of worship. The more well-crafted literary shape and theological content of traditional hymns serve well to capture and instill the whole word of God (Col. 3:16) which is a part of the edification aim of worship. Edification is more than a feeling; it includes instruction. To abandon the use of the traditional is a great deterrent to Christian growth.

Let every voice and instrument praise the Lord. Let every heart and breath behind them give glory to God.

CHAPTER NINE
Rite of Dedication

Brethren churches strive to be faithful in applying the teachings of Holy Scripture in all their practices and policies. According to the teachings of the Bible, our congregations practice *believer's baptism*. That is, the Pastor baptizes youth and adults who make a profession of faith in Jesus Christ as the Savior of their souls and the Lord of their living. Baptism is intended as an outward sign and witness of the believer's inward faith and desire to be a disciple of Jesus (Mt. 3:16; Acts 2:37-41, 8:36-39, 18:7-8; Rom. 6:1-4; Gal. 3:37; Col. 2:9-12; 1 Pet. 3:21). The rite for infants and young children is the act of *consecration or dedication* whereby parents offer their children to God and ask for prayers of blessing and for divine guidance in raising their children in the Christian way. The biblical basis for this practice is the example of Joseph and Mary who *presented* Jesus for consecration at the Temple (Lk. 2:22-23). What follows is an explanation of the significance of the rites in general and of the *Rite of Dedication* in particular.

Signing Belief

The people of God have a long history of "doing things" in the worship setting which not only symbolize their beliefs, but which also help them internalize, activate, and publicize their faith. *Acted signs* help Christians accept responsibility for the faith-life to which they have committed themselves.

Baptism, which implies the use of water, symbolizes identification with the death and resurrection of Jesus. The earliest and truest mode of baptizing was and is immersion of the believer in water as a way of signing three things: the dying [immersion/drowning] and rising [emersion] of Christ; dying to self-centeredness and rising to newness of life; and the purification [cleansing/washing] and forgiveness of the sin condition into which we are all born (Gen. 8:21, Ps. 51:5).

The elements of *Holy Communion/Love Feast* signify for us the attitude of Christ as well as his broken body and shed blood, the ultimate sacrifice for the sins of all who trust in him. When we partake of the elements it is an act of remembrance of Christ's death as a means of proclamation and commemoration to ourselves and others that we take seriously faith in Christ. It is the Christian's special act of thanksgiving. Following the example of Jesus in the Upper Room (John 13), *feetwashing* is a sign of humility, a reminder of the servant nature of Christian discipleship.

Anointing with oil, placed on the head with the sign of the cross, is also an ancient tradition administered at occasions such as the dedication of a child, when asking God's blessing/healing for persons who are seriously ill, and before expected death. Oil was also used for the consecration of Aaron, the first Hebrew priest (Ex. 29:7), when he was set apart for his particular ministry. Samuel anointed David as the future king of Israel (1 Sam. 16:13). A general blessing may be signed through anointing with oil as illustrated in the well-known words of Psalm 23: "Thou anointest my head with oil." Interestingly enough, *Christ* means "anointed one." *Laying on of hands* has also been a sign of consecration and blessing, particularly at dedications, baptisms and ordinations.

At the occasions of these sign-acts there are almost always *three components:* actions, words, and objects. At baptism there is the action of baptizing (submergence and emergence); the words include the threefold formula of "in the name of the Father and of the Son and of the Holy Spirit;" and there is always water used. During our Love Feast/Communion the words of Jesus and/or Paul are spoken, we wash feet and eat; and we use basins, towels, plates and cups with food and drink. For the *Rite of Dedication* there are the words of the vows to which the parents respond as well as the words of consecration by the Pastor; the sign of the cross is administered to the forehead of the child as well as the laying on of hands; and oil is used.

The Dedication of Jesus

In Luke 2:21-24 there are discussed *three long-standing ceremonial acts* important to the Jews which form the basis for the Christian *Rite of Dedication*. First, on the eighth day after birth, a young male was circumcised, the ancient sign of identification for males within the nation

Rite of Dedication

of Israel. At that time the infant's official name was given. Second, after the accepted time of ceremonial purification, thirty-three days more, Joseph and Mary brought Jesus to Jerusalem "to be presented to the Lord." In Exodus 13:2 & 12-16 is described the origins of this practice. God commanded the Israelites to dedicate all males to him in remembrance of their deliverance. When the angel slew all the first-born of Egypt (Ex. 12:29), he spared the first-born sons of Israel. One was given for the other. As a result of this experience, the first-born males were considered the property of God. As an expression of their devotion, the people were to present their sons to God and were permitted to purchase back or redeem them for a nominal price. The ancient offering was five silver shekels, about $2.50. More important that the actual amount of the offering of money was the idea of the ritual which the Israelites held sacred.

The third sacred act was performed about the same time as the offering of the child to God. By custom, forty days following the birth of Jesus was considered a time of purification for the mother. Sometimes the Bible uses the term unclean. Literally it meant she was "not to be touched." The purpose was to force the husband to be gentle and considerate of his wife, particularly during the days immediately following the delivery experience. As a sign of their devotion, after the forty days the law stated they were to offer a year-old lamb as a burnt offering and a young pigeon or dove for a sin offering (Lev. 12:6-7). If a couple could not afford a lamb, they were to bring two doves or two young pigeons instead (Lev. 12:8). In the Luke passage it says Joseph and Mary brought a pair of doves or pigeons since they were poor.

On the spiritual level, these acts illustrated for the Jews the fact of the sinful nature of all human beings and the need for divine grace. All of us are sinners in need of redemption. The price for our salvation is the sacrificed and risen Christ, to whom we surrender our lives by faith. By our trust in him our sin condition is purified, and we are spiritually born anew. Jesus took upon himself our uncleanness though he himself was without spot or blemish (1 Pet. 1:19). Circumcision with naming, the redemption of the first-born, and the purification after childbirth were the three ancient Jewish ceremonies related to infants and their families which form the biblical background and basis for the practice of dedication within the Christian church today.

Administration

After having spoken privately and given instructions to parents regarding the dedication of their child, the family within a public service of worship is invited to the front of the sanctuary where the pastor asks the parents formally if they have come to offer their child to God and seek his blessing that they may be faithful in nurturing their child in the Christian way. Following their affirmation, the pastor may anoint the child on the forehead with oil in the sign of the cross, and then offer a prayer through which, on behalf of the parents and the congregation, the child is offered and dedicated to God's care. The pastor will also pray for the parents that they may be graced with God's Spirit in the care of their child.

Chapter Ten
Signing Repentance

Certain themes come to mind during the Lenten season: Jesus' time in the desert, his ministry, his suffering, confession of sins, sacrifice. At the beginning of this season of the church year is Ash Wednesday. Those in non-prescribed liturgy churches might ask: Why do some churches have a ceremony for the *imposition of ashes?* Why ashes? As a way of approaching the answer to these questions, we will focus on the subject of repentance.

Unlike some other cultures, ours has been traditionally more reserved when it comes to public displays of romantic or religious affections. Of course there is more of each presently, and in the area of romantic affection, the public expressions do not seem many times to be all that wholesome. Some of the public religious expressions are viewed with suspicion. One outward religious expression which has continued in many Christian circles is the imposition of ashes on the forehead on the first day of Lent. It is intended to be a sign of repentance, a humbling of one's self before God, who, in response to Adam's sin, said, as recorded in Genesis 3:19: "Remember, you are dust, and into dust you shall return." The purpose of this rite is to give persons a tangible way of demonstrating sorrow for their sins, their position under a holy and righteous God, and of giving humble thanks for Jesus' sacrifice upon the cross for our sins. Why the ashes? We'll look to a number of scriptures.

For having doubted God, for having questioned God's purposes, his intentions and treatment, Job came to his senses; he realized his sin of pride; he despised himself as the account renders it, and repented in dust and ashes (Job 42:6).

In other Old Testament passages we find additional instances of the use of ashes as a sign of repentance. For example, in chapter 13 of 2 Samuel is given the story of one of the sons of King David, Ammon, who lusted after his sister Tamar. He designed a plot, pretending to be sick in bed, asking that she care for him, which, of course, led to his overpowering her. After the fateful deed, the account reads in verse 19: "Tamar put ashes on her head and tore the ornamented robe she was wearing. She put her hand on her head and went away, weeping aloud as she went." It doesn't say that Ammon put ashes on his head. From our perspective he was the one who should have. Later in revenge, Absalom, Ammon's brother, had some of the king's men execute Ammon.

During the great revival in Israel under Ezra in the fifth century B.C., following the return from Babylonian captivity, the feasts and the reading of the law were restored and the Temple was rebuilt. So moved were the Israelites, and so ashamed of the faithlessness which led to their captivity, they repented. Chapter nine of Nehemiah begins:

> On the twenty-fourth day of [the seventh month], the Israelites gathered together, fasting and wearing sackcloth [a coarsely woven fabric worn to signify mourning and repentance] and having dust on their heads...They stood in their places and confessed their sins and the wickedness of their fathers. They stood where they were and read from the Book of the Law of their God for a quarter of the day, and spent another quarter in confession and in worshiping the Lord their God" (Num. 9:1-3).

In Jeremiah 31:40 we read the prophet speaking of the *valley of ashes*. A solid mound, around five-hundred feet long, two-hundred feet wide, and sixty feet deep, was the ancient dumping place of accumulated ashes, carried out from the Temple sacrifices every evening by Temple staff members. Those who were considered unclean, either by disease or for some act of unfaithfulness, would sit in the ashes.

Psalm 102 is the prayer of a troubled man who mentions ashes.

> Hear my prayer, O Lord; let my cry for help come to you. Do not hide your face from me when I am in distress. Turn your ear to me; when I call, answer me quickly. For my days vanish like smoke; my bones burn like glowing embers. My heart is blighted and withered like grass. I forget to eat food. Because of my loud groaning I am reduced to skin and bones. I am like

a desert owl, like an owl among the ruins I lie awake; I have become like a bird alone on a roof. All day long my enemies taunt me; those who rail against me use my name as a curse. I eat ashes as my food and mingle my drink with tears because of your great wrath. For you have taken me up and thrown me aside. My days are like the evening shadow; I wither away like grass (Ps. 102:1-9).

Jesus mentioned ashes in conjunction with repentance as well. Matthew 11:20-21 says:

> Then Jesus began to denounce the cities in which most of his miracles had been performed, because they did not repent. Woe to you, Korazin! Woe to you Bethsaida! If miracles that were performed in you had been performed in Tyre and Sidon, they would have repented long ago in sackcloth and ashes.

While the use of ashes as a sign of repentance has not been carried over into our culture as a regular practice, the need for repentance remains for all people. For all sin and fall short of the glory of God. How our culture needs to repent from so much unfaithfulness. For only by repentance and faith in Christ may fellowship with God the Father be established or restored.

What is repentance? The Old Testament Hebrew term (*nacham*, e.g. Zech. 8:14) and the New Testament Greek word (*metanoeo*, e.g. Acts 17:30) both mean a change of mind, or to have another mind. They are used to indicate a change of mind with respect to sin, God, and self. Repentance is more than sorrow. We can be sorry for sin; but true repentance, a change of mind and heart, leads to reform. We recall, for example, the stirring words of John the Baptist.

> In those days John the Baptist came, preaching in the Desert of Judea and saying, 'Repent, for the Kingdom of heaven is near.'...People went out to him from Jerusalem and all Judea and the whole region of the Jordan. Confessing their sins, they were baptized by him in the Jordan River (From Mt. 3:1-6).

After his baptism and testing in the wilderness, Jesus began his public ministry. "From that time on Jesus began to preach, 'Repent, for the kingdom of heaven is near'" (Mt. 4:17).

Repentance is important. It's not an easy message to declare or to receive; but it is very important. Repentance is absolutely necessary for there to be a right relationship with God. As Paul said to the elders at Ephesus (Acts 20:21): "I have declared to both Jews and Greeks that they must turn to God in repentance and have faith in our Lord Jesus." Repentance involves *turning from sin and turning to God.* To each of us, to our congregations, to our society, comes the call to repentance.

> Noah's message from the steps going up to the Ark was not, 'Something good is going to happen to you!' Jeremiah was not put into the pit for preaching, 'I'm OK, you're OK!' Daniel was not put into the lion's den for telling people, 'Possibility thinking will move mountains.' John the Baptist was not forced to preach in the wilderness and eventually be decapitated because he [said] 'Smile, God loves you!' The message of these and countless others including our Lord, was simple and profound. Repent.[94]

Before a holy God, we acknowledge our sin. If we wanted to signify our sincerity we could put ashes on our foreheads. If we wanted to demonstrate our humility and reverence for God, we could fall down with our faces to the ground as did and do many Middle Eastern worshipers. Above all, however, we can demonstrate true repentance, not only by confessing sins to God, perhaps even to another person, but more importantly by our reformed conduct. For true repentance involves a change of heart and mind which is then translated into behavior pleasing to God, beneficial for ourselves, and helpful for those around us. John the Baptist underscored the significance of true repentance when he scolded the Pharisees and Sadducees for their hypocrisy. "You brood of vipers! Who warned you to flee from the coming wrath? Produce fruit in keeping with repentance" (Mt. 3:7-8).

---

[94]Green, 302.

In his defense before King Agrippa, the Apostle Paul also sounded this theme. "First to those in Damascus, then to those in Jerusalem and in all Judea, and to the Gentiles also, I preached that they should repent and turn to God and prove their repentance by their deeds. That is why the Jews seized me in the Temple courts and tried to kill me" (Acts 26:20-21).

Application

Psalm 32 is a great source of understanding for the benefits of repentance. In verse five we learn that through repentance our guilt is taken away. Verse seven tells us that through repentance we have protection and deliverance by God. Verse eight indicates wisdom and understanding are imparted. Verse ten says God's love surrounds the repentant person. And in verse eleven we find the repentant one is blessed with a spirit of joy and gladness.

Other scriptures which focus on the values and benefits of repentance include Psalm 103:1-14; and, of course, 1 John 1:9: "If we confess our sins [God] is faithful and just and will forgive us our sins and purify us from all unrighteousness."

As the Old Testament era leaders and prophets called Israel to repentance, so also should we pray that our nation as a whole may turn from the internally destructive moral elements so prevalent everywhere. If as a people we insist on turning our faces away from God's will for human relationships, thought and entertainment, collectively we will reap increasingly what we've sown, what we've permitted to take place before our very eyes. God's word is clear. To Solomon the Lord said: "If my people, who are called by my name, will humble themselves and pray and seek my face and turn from their wicked ways, then will I hear from heaven and will forgive their sin and will heal their land" (2 Chr. 7:14-15). National repentance is needed. It must begin, however, with individual contrition.

Many of us at times may feel like Job. We may not consider ourselves especially wicked, or view ourselves as contributing to the decay of society. And yet that is indication of our failure; for it is our pride which gets translated into a false sense of goodness or superiority, which, in turn, translates into and is manifested in our words, our points of view, and our decisions. Each one of us needs to repent, if not expressed physically, then at least metaphorically and spiritually in dust and ashes; for we are dust and to dust we shall return.

In light of the reason for Jesus' coming and atoning sacrifice, should we not humble ourselves before God, repent of our sins, turn, and keep turning daily to God, that we may share in his good favor, increase in Godliness, and contribute even more meaningfully to his work? Yielding our lives to God's will, living as he desires, will be the truest sign of our repentance, for we know who and what we are, and upon whom we may and must depend. As stanza four of "O Worship the King" declares:

> Frail children of dust, and feeble as frail,
> In Thee do we trust, nor find Thee to fail.
> Thy mercies how tender, how firm to the end,
> Our Maker, Defender, Redeemer, and Friend.

Chapter Eleven
Making a Spiritual Commitment

There are some passages of Scripture with which most people are familiar. For example, the Lord's Prayer (Mt. 6:9-13) is prayed in corporate worship and by individuals in private. At weddings a setting of the prayer is often sung. And at memorial services it is common for the clergy and the people to recite Psalm 23.

If we were to ask what verse of scripture most Christians would cite as foundational to our faith, we would expect many to suggest John 3:16. This verse may be called the hallmark text of Christianity. In a few words it summarizes the plan of God for the salvation of anyone and everyone who surrenders their lives to God by trusting in Jesus Christ as the person of God who died an undeserved death for the expressed purpose of paying the debt we owe God for our sins. *For God so loved the world that he gave his one and only Son, that whoever believes in him shall not perish but have eternal life.*

Whoever believes in him is one of the key expressions which pastors and parishioners use to refer to the call which comes from God through the writers of the Bible to make a spiritual commitment. In the case of John 3:16, the term *believes* refers not simply to acknowledging that Jesus existed, or that he was a great person, or that he died for sinful humanity. The term translated *believes* does not refer merely to intellectual assent or agreement. More importantly and inclusively it refers to *trusting implicitly*. It refers to being related to and having complete confidence in, as you would a best friend, your most trusted companion. When people trust in Christ they are relating to him as their confidante, their advocate and faithful advisor. *Whoever believes* in Jesus means that forgiveness of sins and the gifting of eternal life are granted to those who call upon him and trust him with all their heart, with all their soul, with all their mind, and with all their strength, as the Savior of their souls and the leader of their lives. *Believing* in Jesus, trusting in him, relying on him, his words, his ways, confiding in him, placing one's life in the hands of the one who loved the world so much, surrendering one's life to his directorship, that is what believing in him means, and that is what the Bible teaches we must do in order to be in right relationship with God the Father, to have the fullness of meaning and joy in this life, as well as in the hereafter.

One of the most challenging things to do as Christians is to try to communicate this need, this plan and purpose of God to others. Sometimes, when explaining the Gospel, we may prefer to use certain biblical phrases we've come to associate with making a spiritual commitment. Listeners, however, may not get it, and we may feel we are inadequate and ineffective communicators. Perhaps it would be helpful for us to survey some of the major expressions included in scripture which in one way or another refer to the *making of a spiritual commitment* to God by faith in Jesus.

For example, instead of saying we must *believe in Jesus*, someone may use the phrases, *make a profession of faith in Christ* or *receive Jesus as Savior and Lord*. Another may say we must be *born again*. Still others say we need to be *united with Christ, confess faith in Christ, be saved,* or *be converted*. All of the above are biblical expressions, and all refer to people deciding to commit their lives to the person and ministry of Jesus, appropriating for themselves the person and presence of Christ. It seems to be the case that God inspired the writers of scripture to utilize various expressions because no one phrase in language adequately embraces and conveys all that is meant or involved in making such a commitment, which in our tradition may be made by invitation publicly at the close of a service of worship.

Expressions

Perhaps the most significant as well as the most known expression used is that found in John 3:7: *You must be born again*. The expression may also be rendered *born anew*. The terminology means we must be born a second time, only this time spiritually, inwardly. All of us have been born physically. However, the Bible teaches that all of us came into this world with the same moral tendencies for thinking of self excessively, rather than thinking of God or others, not doing the right thing all of the time (e.g. Ps. 51:5). In other words, we sin (e.g. Rom.

3:23). We come short of what God desires and expects regarding appropriate character. So we must have a God-induced birth of our spirits, that we may be in right relationship with him......Are you born again?

How do persons become born again? Another biblical phrase gives us the answer: by *receiving* the person and Spirit of *Jesus* as the Savior of our souls and Lord of our lives. In John's Gospel we read: *To those who received him, to those who believed in his name, he gave the right to become children of God* (Jn. 1:12-13). In these verses we have three of the expressions Christians use: *believing in Christ, receiving Christ,* and *being born again*, all used synonymously. The Bible tells us we must be born of God spiritually by receiving Jesus, accepting his love and offer of forgiveness of sins. Receiving Jesus means inviting him, through an act of prayer, into one's spiritual heart, into one's life, similarly as you would intentionally invite and receive a guest in your home. In Revelation 3:20 we are given a picture of this. Jesus said: *Here I am! I stand at the door [of your heart] and knock. If anyone opens the door, I will go in and eat with him and he with me.* The Bible says we must invite Jesus into our lives to have fellowship with God. We must receive him as a permanent guest, that he may dwell within us spiritually, and abide with us all our days......Have you received Jesus Christ into your life?

Another scriptural expression, which in part focuses on how we receive or invite the Spirit of Jesus into our lives, is found in Romans 10:9-10. The apostle Paul declared: *If you confess with your mouth 'Jesus is Lord' and believe in your heart that God raised him from the dead, you will be saved.* We receive Jesus into our lives by talking to God, by asking Jesus to come into our lives, and by affirming publicly before our fellows that Jesus is Lord of our lives, that we have and are regularly surrendering our selves to his Lordship, to his directorship, to his leading, to his will and ways. This includes not only saying Jesus is our Savior and Lord, but also believing in our hearts. Needless to say, just expressing commitment outwardly, audibly, is not full commitment. We must believe inwardly. When truly we believe in Jesus inwardly, surrendering our wills to him, inviting him into our lives, we are born again. We have confessed our faith in him. Have you invited, have you received Jesus as the Savior and Lord of your life?

Paul's declaration includes another expression often heard and used, namely *saved*. *If you confess with your mouth 'Jesus is Lord' and believe in your heart that God raised him from the dead, you will be saved.* Saved from what? Saved from the wrath of God, saved from the penalty of un-forgiven sin. God loved the world so much, that he offered his only-begotten Son, that whoever believes in him will not perish, that is, not be cast in the hereafter into utter and eternal separation from God, utter and eternal loneliness and despair, utter and eternal mental and emotional torment, and whatever else is what the Bible refers to as hell. Not confessing and believing in Christ, not being saved doesn't sound like a smart choice to me. Does it to you? Jesus said: ...*I did not come to judge the world, but to save it* (Jn. 12:47b.). And to Timothy Paul wrote: ...*Christ Jesus came into the world to save sinners*...(1 Tim. 1:15) Being saved is not so much something we do, as what God does, and is one of the benefits, one of the results and states of spiritual being and standing with God for inviting Jesus into one's life.......Are you saved?

Other results of receiving Jesus include forgiveness of our sins and his Spirit coming to dwell in our spiritual center. Peter preached: *Repent and be baptized, every one of you, in the name of Jesus Christ for the forgiveness of your sins. And you will receive the gift of the Holy Spirit* (Acts 2:38; see also Jn. 14:15-17, Acts 5:32, Gal. 4:6, 1 Jn. 1:9). Who would not want to be forgiven, freed from the sense of guilt, accepted, pardoned and acquitted, given a new start? By faith in Christ we are forgiven because we've aligned ourselves with the one who satisfied God's standard of righteousness. He paid the debt we owe through his undeserved crucifixion. He offered himself for the sins of anyone and everyone who believes in him.

Who would not want the Spirit of God abiding within our spiritual hearts? With the making of a spiritual commitment to Jesus we have spiritual life! We are born anew inwardly. Paul explained to the Ephesians: *But because of his great love for us, God, who is rich in mercy, made us* [spiritually] *alive with Christ even when we were dead in transgressions--it is by* [God's] *grace you have been saved* (Eph. 2:4-5). And with that life comes spiritual discernment, the ability to recognize, to discern, to distinguish what is of God and what is not (Phil. 1:10, 1 Cor. 2:14). Jesus' Spirit living within our spirits gives us the sensitivity for appropriate thought and behavior. We have a new start in life (Jn. 3:3), a renewed mindset (Rom. 12:2, 2 Cor. 3:18), a new attitude (Eph. 4:23), inner peace (Rom. 5:2), joy and hope (Rom. 15:3), and the promise of life with God forever (Jn. 3:16). With all of the ache in peoples' lives, who wouldn't want the benefits of genuine commitment to Jesus?

> Have you trusted in Christ? Do you believe in him? Are you born again? Have you received Jesus into your life as your personal Savior and Lord? Have you confessed him with your mouth and believed in your heart? Do you know you are saved from the wrath of God? Do you know the inner joy of Christ living within?

If your response is *no* to the above, then what possible excuse could you give God, standing before him, which could be acceptable or possible? Following your death, when you stand before the Creator of the universe, and you are faced with the judgment of God upon your life, will you be able to respond affirmatively to the following questions?

> Did you do as my word declared and the preachers you heard explained? Did you accept my offer of salvation through trusting in Jesus? Did you trust him as your Savior? Did you confess him as Lord of your life and really mean it? Are you born again?

How do you think you might feel to stand before the one in whose hands is your fate forever, and say *No, I did not*? Why, you would shudder with a terror and fear indescribable. We don't know when the life we live will draw to a close. And when it does, could we face God confidently? Could *you* face God with the assurance of having received Jesus as your Savior and Lord?

In the variety of ways the scriptures present, we must come to terms with our true selves, our spirituality, our relationship with the one ultimately to whom we owe our existence, and the one whom we must thank or reject for the offer of redemption. We cannot include God in our lives on our terms. It must be on his.

To put it yet in another way, the Bible says there must be a change within us. We must turn from our self-centered orientation to a God and others orientation. We must turn from self and turn to God, what the Bible refers to as being *converted* (Mt. 18:3, Acts 4:19, 15:3, 1 Tim. 3:6). A change must take place, a birth of the spirit, by receiving Jesus as Savior and Lord.

> Have you made the turn? Have you experienced a change?
> Are you united with Jesus by faith (Rom. 6:5, 1 Cor. 6:17, Phil. 2:1)?

Again, if your response is negative, then I encourage you from a genuine and urgent love to surrender your life to Christ, to settle the matter, to *make a spiritual commitment*, to receive him into your life. You might pray the following:

> Eternal God, I confess my sins to you. I am in great spiritual need. I desire to be born anew. I invite and receive the Spirit of Jesus into my life as the Savior of my soul and the Lord of my living. Thank you for forgiving me and living within me. Help me to be faithful. I pray in the name of Jesus. Amen.

CHAPTER TWELVE
Rites of Christian Baptism and Confirmation

Sign-Acts of Faith

Baptism has been practiced for many centuries in Christian churches, ever since Jesus commissioned the disciples to "go and make disciples of all nations, baptizing them in the name of the Father and of the Son and of the Holy Spirit..." (Mt. 28:19). The practice of baptism is understood through an examination of a wide variety of scriptures. We're going to ask and answer four questions: from where did the practice of baptism come; why are people baptized today; what are the meanings attached to Christian baptism; and what are some values of participating in the baptismal action?

Antecedents of Christian Baptism

From where did the practice of baptism arise? Baptism (Gk. *baptizo*) has its roots in the Jewish observance of the Day of Atonement, also known as *Yom Kippur*, observed by Jews usually in September each year. On the Day of Atonement, dating back to the days of Moses and Aaron, sacrifices were offered for the forgiveness of sins. As recorded in Leviticus 16, Aaron the priest was instructed to offer sacrifices for himself, his household, and for all the people. A part of the ceremony included Aaron *bathing* himself before putting on sacred garments (4:4, 24). Those who assisted Aaron had to bathe themselves before they performed their duties. Their *washing* was a sign of purification before performing holy acts before a holy God. The idea of a *purification bath*, therefore, dated far back into Israel's history.

By the time of Jesus, new converts to Judaism were baptized, a term which means to be *immersed* in water, as an act of *self-dedication* to the God of Israel. Although not mentioned in scripture, we know from Jewish historical documents that proselyte baptism was a custom during the first century after Jesus for the purpose of symbolizing purification from heathen pollution. To be sure, before the ministry of Jesus, John, his cousin, forever known as the Baptist, was the voice in the desert calling people, both Jews and Gentiles, to repentance. His was a baptism of repentance for forgiveness of sins (Mt. 3:1-6, Lk. 3:3). Matthew 3:6 says: "Confessing their sins, they were baptized by him in the Jordan River." John's baptism carried with it the understanding of moral change. In other words, there was an *ethical significance* attached to the significance of the rite. When persons submitted to John's baptism they were committing themselves to behaving in a more Godly fashion. This is understood by John's strong remark to the Pharisees and Sadducees: "You brood of vipers! Who warned you to flee from the coming wrath? Produce fruit in keeping with repentance" (Mt. 3:7-8).

We learn from the Gospels that it was John who was asked by Jesus to administer our Lord's baptism. John was reluctant because he knew Jesus did not need to repent of sins. Nor was Jesus a Gentile converting to Judaism; he did not need to be purified. And yet, Jesus submitted to the baptismal action. He said: "… it is proper for us to do this to fulfill all righteousness" (Mt. 3:15). What did Jesus mean by this? Theologians have debated the reason for Jesus' baptism. Of the following I believe we may be certain. First, in his baptism Jesus was setting an example for all who would desire to be in right relationship with God. Second, in baptism Jesus was submitting himself to the will of the Father. And third, Jesus' baptism was a formal beginning to his ministry, an action of consecration and strengthening, for we read in Matthew 3:16 that the Spirit of God endowed him in a special way at his baptism. So the baptismal action is, at the very least, a *sign-action* which is accompanied by the special endowment of the Holy Spirit.

Our first question was: From where did the practice of baptism come? The practice has its roots in the Levitical Day of Atonement ceremony of ritual purification bathing. Christian baptism was immediately preceded by Jewish proselyte baptism for self-dedication and purification; by John's baptism of repentance; and by Jesus' example. Why people are baptized today is, in part, similar to the reason for Jewish proselyte baptism. That is, when persons become converts to

Christianity, they are baptized. Baptism was and is an initiation rite. All of the above meanings, including self-dedication, purification, repentance, moral responsibility, and the filling of the Holy Spirit seem to be operative in Christian baptism in some fashion. However, we need to examine more fully the New Testament material to understand what developed into and came to be understood as the Christian practice and significance of baptism. And so we may ask: Why are people baptized today?

Purpose of Christian Baptism

The primary purpose of Christian baptism is to *sign union with Jesus Christ*. To say it another way, in Christian baptism persons sign the death and resurrection of Jesus whom they choose to pledge their allegiance and follow. Baptism is the action Jesus and the disciples chose which would best convey the atonement actions of Jesus on our behalf, that is, his death and resurrection. One source is the sixth chapter of Romans. After having presented a lengthy discussion that it is by faith in Christ that people are redeemed, Paul admonished the Roman Christians to live as though they were indeed redeemed. If they *professed* to be united with Christ by their faith, they should *act* by faith in ways which exemplified transformation of character. Paul cited their baptism as a picture of that union with Christ. He wrote: "Don't you know that all of us who were baptized into Christ Jesus were baptized into his death? We were therefore buried into death in order that, just as Christ was raised from the dead through the glory of the Father, we too may live a new life. If we have been united with him like this in his death, we will certainly also be united with him in his resurrection" (Rom. 6:3-5). Spiritual union with Christ is that which believers experience when they invite the Spirit of Christ into their lives by faith and prayer. That union is symbolized in the baptismal act. The actions of *immersion and submersion* in water symbolize the *dying and death* of Jesus as the atonement for the sins of all who trust in him by faith. The action of *emergence* from the water symbolizes the *rising and resurrection* of Jesus, a physical picture and foreshadowing of the resurrection promised for believers at the second coming of Jesus (see also Col. 2:12).

Therefore, by *faith inwardly* and by *baptism outwardly* we are united with Christ in his death and resurrection.

Additionally, baptism is a *public response*, a demonstration and a testimony of one's faith in Christ. In Acts 8:26-29 we find the story of the Apostle Philip who shared the good news of Christ with an Ethiopian, after which it says that they went down into the water and Philip baptized him. The gospel was shared, the Ethiopian believed, and then he was baptized, a response, a testimony to his faith. Again, in Acts 16:29-34, we read of the jailor who was converted by the ministry of Paul and Silas. They shared the good news of salvation by faith in Jesus with the jailor and his family, after which it says they believed and were baptized. That is the biblical pattern (see also Acts 18:7-8 & 19:1-6).

Our second question was: Why are people baptized today? The answer is to *give witness to their union with Jesus Christ*. Baptism is a sign-action response to and a visualization of the act of atonement accomplished by Jesus, to whom believers are united by inward faith.

Other Meanings in Scripture

Our third question was: What meanings are attached to Christian baptism? In addition to the primary meaning, *union with Christ*, baptism signs *new life*, abundant life now as well as in the afterlife. By faith in the crucified and risen Christ, the sin condition with which we were born was nailed to the cross. It was absorbed by our Savior, forgiven, sent away. The grip and mastery of sin for believers was shattered. By faith in Christ, sin no longer has to dominate, because the Holy Spirit, who is imparted through our union with Christ, gives believers capacity and the resources to combat the temptations and allurements of the world. Paul wrote in Romans 6: "For we know that our old self was crucified with him...that we should no longer be slaves to sin...but alive to God..." (from Rom. 6:4-14). By *plunging* ourselves into the death and resurrection of Jesus, we are delivered from the clutches and ultimate consequences of unforgiven sin. Baptism, therefore, is a picture of the new life believers possess in the present, as well as a dramatization of the future resurrection. It is a picture of dying, drowning to sin's grip, and of rising, breathing again to a new quality of life. Baptism is a sign of new life.

Rites of Christian Baptism and Confirmation

Baptism is also a symbol of *cleansing*. We often refer to the observances of baptism and Holy Communion as rites (L. *ritus*), meaning ceremonies which attach spiritual significance to familiar objects and actions. In Holy Communion we use bread and beverage and we eat and drink. Baptism uses water and employs the action of bathing. The most basic of images presented in baptism, therefore, is cleansing. In baptism *we sign outwardly the cleansing of the grip of sin which is made possible inwardly by the Spirit of Jesus. Outward cleansing signs inward forgiveness.* Are believers sinless? No. But positionally under God they are viewed as forgiven. Does that forgiveness give us the freedom to sin? Of course not. It gives us the desire, the freedom and the power of God to want to strive to live a new life for God, because we are so thankful for his love and mercy.

By mentioning the work of the Spirit, we've introduced the third additional meaning of baptism: *the endowment of the Holy Spirit.* It is the presence of God's Spirit in the inner being which enables persons to be in union with Christ. It is God's Spirit which gives us the power to live a new life. It is the Holy Spirit who delivers us from the bondage to sin and lifts believers to a new and higher plane of Godly thinking and living. And it is the power of God's Spirit which will transform our lowly bodies to be like Christ's glorious body (e.g. Phil. 3:21).

In Acts 2:38f. we read that Peter preached: "Repent and be baptized, every one of you, ...for the forgiveness of your sins. And you will receive the gift of the Holy Spirit." Following persons' sincere expressions of repentance of sins and profession of faith in Jesus as the Savior of their souls and the Lord of their living, the Holy Spirit of God comes to dwell within the heart of the believer. The coming of the Spirit in a special way is symbolized by the *laying on of hands* following baptism, and by *signing with oil* the cross of Christ upon the forehead (see also Acts 10:44-48 & 19:5-6). In The Brethren Church these actions immediately following the administration of baptism are the *Rite of Confirmation*, signing the coming of the Spirit in power.

An additional fourth meaning of baptism is *discipleship*. Just as Jesus was baptized as the first act of his formal ministry for our redemption, so also baptism is viewed as the first *formal action of believers* regarding their *discipleship*. As such, baptism is a sign of commitment to Christ and his ministry.

Our third question was: What meanings are attached to Christian baptism? The answers are: union with Christ, new life, cleansing, endowment with the Holy Spirit, and discipleship. All of these meanings are a part of baptism as the initiation rite of Christian discipleship, the act of *public response* of persons who profess faith in Jesus Christ.

Values of Participation

Our last question is: What are the values of participating in the act of baptism? In addition to those given above, here we focus on the practical benefits of the physical action of being baptized. We are all aware of the educational value of learning by doing. Learning is usually more genuine and long-lasting when students participate in a drama or role play situation. So also with baptism. Our Lord and the early church knew full well the importance of having a way of enacting the sacrifice of atonement, to enable believers not only to remember what Jesus accomplished for us, but more importantly here to impress upon us the sacred meanings attached to the rite. The action of being baptized helps believers understand and internalize the death and resurrection of Jesus. It helps candidates simulate personal contact with the redeeming actions of Jesus, and, therefore, come into closer contact with him. Moreover, because the action is a public one, believers come to realize they are being identified with and are a part of a larger body of Christians, the Church of Jesus Christ. Through union with Jesus, believers are united with all others who have made the same spiritual commitment, with all who are taking the same life-long journey of striving to emulate the character of Christ, and sharing with others, in word and deed, the good news of our Savior.

As a sign-act of faith, baptism is a sign of the atonement made by Jesus' death and resurrection; a sign of commitment and obedience; a sign of self-dedication; a sign of repentance; a sign of ethical change; a sign of new life and the promise of our resurrection; a sign of endowment with the Holy Spirit; and a sign of discipleship. Needless to say, after becoming aware of such meaningfulness, baptism is not to be taken lightly. All who truly repent of their sins and invite the Spirit of Jesus into their hearts are encouraged to follow through with the example of our Savior and welcome the blessings of Christian baptism.

Administration

When persons have made a profession of faith and indicate their desire to be baptized, the pastor visits with them individually to discuss the significances of the rites of baptism and confirmation and the administration of them. In a public service of worship, whether within or at the close of a Sunday morning service or within a separate service specifically devoted to the baptism of persons, individuals enter the baptismal tank or other body of water in which they are asked to kneel. The pastor asks them if they have acknowledged Jesus Christ as their Savior and Lord. Upon the positive affirmation of their commitment, the pastor, perhaps holding one arm and placing his other hand on the candidate's back, immerses them, the candidates bending forward from the waist. The *baptizands* in Brethren churches are immersed three times (triune immersion), once for each person of the Godhead. "I baptize you in the name of the Father and of the Son and of the Holy Spirit" (Mt. 28:19).

When the candidates rise for the third time, they are asked to stand, whereupon the pastor anoints their foreheads with oil with the sign of the cross symbolizing and, therefore, *confirming* their being anointed by the Holy Spirit. The deacons of the church may then join the pastor and the candidates to lay hands on their head or shoulder and offer prayers, praying for God's Spirit to come upon them in a special way, empowering them for Christian discipleship.

Chapter Thirteen
Church and Membership

The name Jonathan Edwards is forever etched in the history of Christianity. His sermon, "Sinners in the Hands of An Angry God," is perhaps the most famous of any American clergyman. Edwards served the Congregational Church of Northampton, Massachusetts for twenty-three years, beginning his tenure there in 1726 as the Assistant Minister to his grandfather, the Rev. Solomon Stoddard. In 1729 after fifty-seven years as Pastor of the church, Solomon Stoddard died, and Jonathan Edwards became the church's Pastor, a post he held until 1750. The story of the dismissal of this greatest American theologian is well-known and has relation to the present topic.

It seems that Edwards' predecessor held the view that persons may apply for church membership if they were seeking Christianity and desiring to follow in the Christian way, even without formally making a profession of personal faith in Jesus Christ as Savior and Lord. That policy, which may seem strange to us, was in place for many years, and Edwards went with the flow, honoring his grandfather's views and the people who were received into membership during the previous years. "In December 1748," however, "Edwards had told an applicant for membership that he must profess to be a Christian before he could become a communicant. After consultation with others, the individual refused...The report of this, says Edwards, 'made great uneasiness in the town'."[95] Edwards, after careful study of scripture, had become increasingly uncomfortable with his grandfather's position on membership, a position which was the practice throughout the New England colonies. Without going into all the troubling details over the next two years, the congregation would not bend or listen to Edwards' biblical defense, and they officially asked him to leave in 1750.

We may ask fairly: What does the Bible teach regarding what is the

---

[95] Iain H. Murray, *Jonathan Edwards: A New Biography* (Edinburgh: The Banner of Truth Trust, 1987), 316.

Church, or rather who are the Church; and, therefore, who may be members of local churches? As a help to prospective and current church members alike, whom we receive formally in the context of a worship service, we will discuss these matters, then offer several significances of local church membership.

The Church

The word *church* in the New Testament comes from the Greek, *ekklesía*, which means literally an assembly, congregation, or collection of persons "called out" (e.g. Acts 20:28, Eph. 1:22). The term is used without distinction to size. It is found to be used with reference to a multitude (e.g. Acts 2:41, 47) or a gathering of believers in a home (Rom. 16:5). Dutch theologian James Arminius (1560-1609) defined the Christian Church as a congregation of all the believers who have been called out of every tongue, tribe, people, nation and station in life "by the saving [work] of God from the state of corruption to the dignity of the sons of God through the Gospel, and are by a true faith engrafted into Christ, as living members are to the Head, to the praise and the glorious grace of God (Mt. 5:15-16, Acts 4:31, 1 Pet. 2:9-10, Rom. 8:28-30, Rom. 6:5, Eph. 3:17, 30)."[96] Why is this so? Because the purpose of God is to make forgiveness of sins, reconciliation to God and eternal life available to all. Because of God's love for his creation, through the Church humanity is called to faith in Jesus as the atonement for sins. Those persons, all over the world, who respond affirmatively to the call, are pronounced *not guilty* for their sins. They are *justified* in God's sight to inherit eternal life. They are referred to in the Bible as the *elect* (e.g. 1 Pet. 1:1, 2 Pet. 1:10). They are the ones who are *called-out*. They are the true Church.[97]

When we observe how the Church exists in the world, however, we see that the called-out-ones gather together in groups in many locations

---

[96]James Nicols and William Nicols, trans. *The Works of James Arminius* (Grand Rapids: Baker Book House, 1991), Vol. 2, 246.

[97]Arminius also defined the Church as: "A congregation of [people] called forth by God, out of their own nature, into the supernatural dignity of adoption as sons of God to his glory, and of those who answer this call of God." *The Works of James Arminius*, Vol. 2, 245.

for worship, to hear the reading and preaching of the Scriptures, to be baptized, to receive the elements of Holy Communion, to study together, and to serve. It is helpful, therefore, to think of the Church in two ways, both *invisible* and *visible*.

The Church Invisible

By the Church *invisible* is meant the worldwide congregation of all true believers. *Globally*, all those who have accepted the call of God to believe in Jesus Christ as their Savior and Lord, and whose spiritual lives, therefore, have been *regenerated* by the work of the Holy Spirit, are the Church. We may not see them all at once, and they are not all gathered in one place, thus we refer to them as the Church invisible. Yet all together they are the Church of Jesus Christ on planet Earth. The Church invisible, therefore, is a synonym for the worldwide body of believers in Jesus. It is the sum total of all *regenerate* persons, all who have believed in Christ in their hearts since his first coming, and all who will believe in him until the resurrection at his second coming (Lk. 14:14, Jn. 5:28-29 & 6:40, Acts 24:15, 1 Cor. 15:52, Rev. 20:5-6).

John Wesley described the invisible Church as all persons in the *universe* whom God has called out of the world to be one body, united by the one Holy Spirit of God, having one common faith, the same hope of eternal life, one God and Father who is above all and in them all.[98] Theologian Louis Berkhof (1873-1957) wrote: "The essence of the Church is to be found in the sphere of the invisible: in faith, communion with Christ, and in participation in the blessing of salvation through the Holy Spirit...The really important thing for [us] is that [we] belong to the spiritual or invisible Church; but this is closely connected with membership in the visible Church."[99]

The Church Visible

The visible, external and institutional Church is the Church seen. In the words of John Calvin: "Wherever we see the Word of God pure-

---

[98]From Wesley's sermon, "Of the Church," in *The Works of John Wesley* (Grand Rapids: Baker Book House, 1991), Vol. VI, 395-396.

[99]Louis Berkhof, *The History of Christian Doctrine* (Grand Rapids: Baker Book House, 1975), 236.

ly preached and heard, and the sacraments administered according to Christ's institution, there, it is not to be doubted, a Church of God exists."[100] In this regard we recall the words of Jesus: "Where two or three are gathered in my name, there am I in the midst of them" (Mt. 18:20). The Church visible is a group of persons who profess faith in Christ and gather in a particular location to hear the scriptures read and interpreted, to be baptized and to receive the Lord's Supper. These are some of the primary externals, the marks of the Church visible. These are the outward signs for the recognition of a church gathered.

Why do we gather in groups? Because the visible Church exists to provide external helps for the production of faith in people's hearts. Ministers of the Gospel preach and call people to faith in Christ, to make known the wisdom and Word of God (Eph. 3:10). Following the charge of Jesus to the disciples, we preach the Gospel in order to make disciples, to baptize them in the name of the Father and of the Son and of the Holy Spirit (Mk. 16:15, Mt. 28:19-20), and to teach them. Through worship, preaching and teaching, the visible Church helps Christians to increase and mature in faith and faith-living. By the authority given them in the scriptures, pastors administer the rites which foster and strengthen faith.[101]

In the Bible the Church is often referred to as the *Body of Christ*. With reference to the Church invisible Paul wrote: "...through the gospel the Gentiles are heirs together with Israel, members together of one body, and sharers in the promise of Christ Jesus" (Eph. 3:6). Speaking of Jesus Paul said: "He is the head of the body, the church; he is the beginning and the firstborn from among the dead, so that in everything he might have the supremacy" (Col. 1:18). Christ is the head and the connecting link of the worldwide invisible Church. However, most often in Paul's letters is the *Body of Christ* imagery used to describe the Church visible (Rom. 12:4-6, 1 Cor. 12:12-13). R.C. Sproul explained: "The church is not so much an organization as it is an organism...Just as a human body is organized to function in unity by

---

[100]McNeill, *Calvin: Institutes of the Christian Religion*, Book IV, Chapter 1, Section 9, 1023.

[101]Ibid., Book IV, Chapter 1, Section 1, 1012.

the co-working and codependence of many parts, so the church as a body displays unity and diversity. Though ruled by one head, Christ, the body has many members, each gifted and endowed by God to contribute to the work of the whole body."[102] Someone has explained:

> In any flesh-and-bones body, there are a variety of cells. There are nerve cells, blood cells, and many others, each having a distinct function. The body operates smoothly, not because the cells get together and vote on what to do, but because each one does what it was designed to do. It is the function of the head to bring all these different functions together, so that the body operates effectively as each cell gives itself to the task of functioning according to its design. Certainly the body would not operate properly if its cells chose to go their own way. Do you know what we call a rebellion of the cells of your stomach? We call it indigestion! A revolt of your brain cells is called insanity. Any time cells in our body don't operate properly, it means that the body is sick, that something is wrong with it. Many of the problems in the church are a result of our forgetting that the church is a body with a head, Jesus Christ. Instead we sometimes try to operate the church as an organization. As a result, the church has no more power than any other human organization at work in the world.[103]

We gather in groups to pool our personal and collective abilities and resources to accomplish the work of Christ effectively. In the visible church, members are encouraged to use whatever interests and abilities with which God has blessed them for the good of the whole body. As an organism it is their responsibility to work together in the ministry of Christ, to support one another. Paul wrote: "From him the whole body joined and held together by every supporting ligament, grows and builds itself up in love, as each part does its work" (Eph. 4:16).

For safety reasons, mountain climbers rope themselves together

---

[102]R. C. Sproul, *Essential Truths of the Christian Faith* (Wheaton, Illinois: Tyndale House Publishers, Inc., 1992), 218.
[103]Green, 67.

when climbing a mountain. That way, if one climber should slip and fall, he would not fall to his death. He would be held by the others until he could regain his footing. The church ought to be like that. When one member slips and falls, the others should hold him up until he regains his footing. We are all roped together by the Holy Spirit.[104]

Moreover, Christ determined that some of the body would be leaders, pastors and teachers, "to prepare God's people for works of service, so that the body of Christ may be built up until we all reach unity in the faith and in the knowledge of the Son of God and become mature, attaining to the whole measure of the fullness of Christ" (Eph. 4:11-13).

At one of the banks where my wife worked, an undocumented handout entitled "Lessons from Geese" was circulated to the employees to emphasize the values of working together. There are striking parallels to the visible Church. The following are the five facts and lessons included.

FACT 1: As each goose flaps its wings it creates an "uplift" for the birds that follow. By flying in a "V" formation the whole flock adds 71% greater flying range than if each bird flew alone.

LESSON 1: People who share a common direction and sense of community can get where they are going quicker and easier because they are traveling on the thrust of one another.

FACT 2: When a goose falls out of formation, it suddenly feels the drag and resistance of flying alone. It quickly moves to the back into formation to take advantage of the lifting power of the bird immediately in front of it.

LESSON 2: If we have as much sense as a goose we stay in formation with those headed where we want to go. We are willing to accept their help and give our help to others.

FACT 3: When the lead goose tires, it rotates back into formation and another goose flies to the point position.

---

[104]Ibid., 66.

LESSON 3: It pays to take turns doing the hard tasks and sharing leadership. As with geese, people are interdependent on each other's skills, capabilities, and unique arrangements of gifts, talents or resources.

FACT 4: The geese flying in formation honk to encourage those up front to keep up their speed.

LESSON 4: We need to make sure our honking is encouraging. In groups where there is encouragement, the production is much greater. The power of encouragement (to stand by one's heart or core values, and encourage the heart and core of others) is the quality of honking we seek.

FACT 5: When a goose gets sick, wounded or shot down, two geese drop out of formation and follow it down to help and protect it. They stay with it until it dies or is able to fly again. Then, they launch out with another formation or catch up with the flock.

LESSON 5: If we have as much sense as geese, we will stand by each other in difficult times as well as when we are strong.

Needless to say, we should do everything possible to provide brotherly and sisterly concern, support, and responsibility for one another as the visible Church. We must do all we can to carry each other along in the journey of faith, enabling each one to be and do all that is possible, not only for the well-being of each one, but also for the flourishing and accomplishments of the whole local body of believers, the gathered flock of God.

Criteria for Membership

Accepting the above as a fair understanding of the church, invisible and visible, we deduce that the criteria by which persons may be received into membership of the local church is that they are first and foremost true believers in Jesus Christ, that is, members of the invisible Church. While we would not pretend to be the ultimate judges of this, for that is God's domain, it is our responsibility to ask persons if they have made a profession of faith in Jesus or lead them to do so, and to instruct them regarding Christian baptism as the way Jesus taught new believers are to demonstrate their identity and allegiance with our Lord, and as their first official act of Christian discipleship. What we are saying is, that persons who become members of a local visible church must first be members of the Church invisible. There must be an equivalency in this, because there is and must be a close connection between the two. This may seem strange to mention. However, in some churches, there may not be as much care as there should be in screening persons. Not to do so is to invite and create a weak membership, which then will most likely lead to a lack of support regarding accomplishing the church's goals, ministries, and securing finances. We have an obligation to welcome into local church membership only those who profess their faith in Jesus as their personal Savior and Lord. Hopefully, after having become acquainted for a time before receiving persons, the example of the prospective members will have indicated the sincerity of their profession, thus enabling churches to be as confident as possible that their welcoming is based on genuineness of commitment.

To repeat, the basic requirement for being a Christian, namely making a personal commitment to Jesus as Savior and Lord, which results in one becoming a part of the global invisible church of all true believers, is the basic requirement for persons affiliating with a local, visible congregation of Christians. Anything less than the basic requirement would be ridiculous, totally illogical and without biblical support.

It is interesting to note that a few short years after Jonathan Edwards was dismissed from the pastorate in Northampton, other clergy had followed his lead and influenced their congregations sufficiently so that all Congregational churches in New England either adopted the teaching that persons applying for membership must make a public profession of faith in Christ, or they became Unitarian.[105]

Reviewing, probing further, and saying this even in another way: Could a person be a Christian, a "member" of the invisible church, without being an official member of the visible church? We would have to say, yes. Could a person become an official member of a visible, local

---

[105]Murray, 472.

congregation without being a "member", that is, a born-again believer in Jesus, in the invisible church? The answer must be an emphatic, no! There must be an equivalency of the two. One must *be* one in order to be *in* the other. Again, is it possible in the most basic of terms to be born-again believers without being an officially recognized member of a local visible congregation of Christians? *Of course.* However, we must be quick to ask: Is it appropriate and acceptable for someone to make a profession of faith in Jesus and not get involved or choose to be an active member of a local church? Absolutely not. The Bible offers sufficient evidence which suggests even early Christians made commitments not only to Jesus as Savior and Lord, but they also made commitments to a particular body of believers with whom they would assume their responsibilities as followers of Jesus.

Commitments

Following a stirring explanation of the events in which the Holy Spirit was poured out upon believers, the apostle Peter declared that believers should repent of their sins and be baptized (Acts 2:38). Verse forty-one then says: "Those who accepted his message were baptized, and about three thousand were added to their number that day." Notice that this verse refers to the basic requirement for being a Christian and a part of the invisible church of Jesus Christ. It speaks of accepting Peter's proclamation of the Gospel message for themselves, and then publicly giving witness to that intentional and genuine commitment by identifying with Jesus in his death and resurrection through participation in the baptismal actions of immersion and emergence from water.

Then verse forty-two indicates what followed their commitment to Christ: "They devoted themselves to the apostles' teaching and to the fellowship, to the breaking of bread and to prayer." In this summary description of the new believers' activities immediately following their conversion, we learn that they committed themselves not only to the study of and adherence to the content of the faith as given by the apostles, they also committed themselves to the *group*, the fellowship, to one another, to that visible local body of believers with whom they would share in the observance of the bread and the cup to intentionally and regularly remember Jesus' sacrifice for their sins,[106] and to praying together.

To reiterate and emphasize the point, they committed themselves to Jesus, and then they committed themselves to one another and to the body of truth of the faith. They were committed to Christ, and they were committed to the people of Christ, the visible church in that place, who would be doing the work of Christ. Their commitment to Jesus and to the group and its activities and purposes is strong biblical support for our present day practice of requiring for formal admittance into a local church's membership a public profession of faith in Jesus and an expression of pledge to be faithful to the local church's people and ministries.

Significances

What are some significances of pledging faithfulness to the local church family and work? When people join civic organizations or clubs of various sorts, they are asked questions which indicate their support for the group and its goals, and/or they are required to pay dues, which convey hopefully the same commitment, otherwise, theoretically, they would not make the financial contribution. In other words, most groups have some kind of *initiation requirement.* The same has been in the church for many centuries. There must be expressed commitment to the group and its goals in order to ensure the goals will be reached and effectively. Rick Warren, in his book *The Purpose Driven Life,* affirms what we have been saying.

> The difference between being a church attender and a church member is commitment. Attenders are spectators from the sidelines; members get involved in the ministry. Attenders are consumers; members are contributors. Attenders want the benefits of a church without sharing the responsibility. They are like couples who want to live together without committing to a marriage....The Christian life is more than just commitment to Christ; it includes a commitment to other Christians...You

---

[106]The "breaking of bread" was a common and abbreviated biblical phrase referring to taking the bread and the cup of Holy Communion.

become a Christian by committing yourself to Christ, but you become a *church member* by committing yourself to a specific group of believers.[107]

One of the early Puritans was John Winthrop (1588-1649), the first Governor of the Massachusetts Bay Colony. He delivered a sermon, "A Model of Christian Charity," while on board ship in Salem Harbor just before landing in 1630. In his message he said: "We must delight in each other, make others conditions our own, rejoyce together, mourn together, labor and suffer together, always having before our eyes our community, as members of the same body."[108] The point is made. When we make a personal commitment to Jesus, we become a part of God's household (Eph. 2:19), God's redeemed family, wherever they may be. In the outward expression of water baptism we give witness to that union with Christ, who died and rose from the dead. Baptism is our first act of Christian discipleship. It is a sign and an initiation rite of our inclusion in the global invisible Church. We're a part of the Kingdom of God, the Body of Christ. However, the truth is we cannot discover where we fit and how we may be useful in the Body, and we cannot contribute to Christ's work as fully or effectively, or even grow spiritually as God intends unless we align ourselves officially with a particular local body of believers; because personal growth and the ministry of the Church are accomplished in the community setting, not in isolation. As members of a local church we accept and assume our responsibility as Christian disciples. As Acts 2:42 indicates, we choose to be committed to a particular group with whom we desire to be affiliated, and through whom we will live out our discipleship.

More than that, as Ephesians 5:21 says, "Submit to one another out of reverence for Christ," we are to commit to a particular local church that we may be held accountable for our responsibility to live and grow spiritually and to be involved in the ministry which Jesus commissioned

---

[107] Rick Warren, *The Purpose Driven Life* (Grand Rapids: Zondervan, 2002), 136-137 [Large Print Edition, 171-172]. See also his *Purpose Driven Church*, 1995, also by Zondervan, 309-392, for an extended discussion on church membership.

[108] Sermon quoted in Edmund S. Morgan, ed. *Puritan Political Ideas, 1588-1794* (Indianapolis: Bobbs-Merrill, 1965), 92.

his disciples to publicize the Gospel, to make disciples, and to teach them to be obedient to the person and instruction of Jesus (Acts 28:19-20).

Therefore, within the context of a public service of worship as an initiation rite for commitment to the local Church, we ask the following questions publicly as *vows* of church membership:

Have you received Jesus Christ as your personal Savior and Lord?

Will you uphold this congregation and its work with your *prayers*; with your *presence* in worship, study opportun-ities, and other activities and functions; with your *gifts*; and with your *service*, all as God enables you?

Upon the positive responses to these questions of pledge, individuals are formally received and welcomed as members of the particular congregation of believers. They may then hold office, teach, and vote.

To review, Acts 2:41, which says, "Those who accepted his message were baptized, and about three thousand were added to their number that day," speaks to the basic requirement to be a Christian, namely, commitment to Jesus. Acts 2:42, which says, "They devoted themselves to the apostles' teaching and to the fellowship...," emphasizes what naturally follows commitment to Christ, that is, commitment to a specific group of Christians, and to spiritual disciplines such as study, observing Holy Communion and praying. Then, of course, the passage goes on to say they pooled their resources (Acts 2:44-45). As with the difference between co-habitation and marriage, so also people may attend a particular church; but unless they accept the vows of loyalty and commitment and responsibility, the relationship is not fully consummated. There's something about saying "I do" or "I promise" in public, which settles the matter. Without formal membership and commitment to one another, people are more likely not to grow spiritually or serve as they are expected by God to do, because they lack the interaction, encouragement and support of a group.

Moreover, we do not grow or accomplish ministry in isolation, for we are interdependent of one another in life in general, and in the church in particular, and we are mutually dependent upon God. We should do all we can to bring health to the collective nature of life and the Church. As with registering to vote and actually voting, in church membership we accept the responsibility for nurturing and preserving the interdependent fabric and activity of the church, for "we are members one of another" (Eph. 4:25).

Furthermore, in the New Testament era, as the Church grew and spread, local churches were established, as in the churches at Ephesus, Philippi and Colosse; and there was discipline enforced for false teaching, for disruptive behavior, and for immoral conduct.[109] If there were no official membership requirements, then discipline would not need to have been mentioned or enforced as it was.

To review and summarize: In *profession of faith* we accept the *Saviorship* and commit ourselves to the person of Jesus. In *baptism* we accept the *Lordship* and surrender ourselves to the teaching and instruction of Jesus. In *church membership* we accept and commit ourselves to the *ministry of Jesus*, to the *core beliefs* of the faith, and to the *people* of that congregation with whom the ministry will be accomplished. Local church membership is both a sign and a means of accepting the responsibilities of being a Christian.

Preparation

The church of the New Testament was the church of our foundations. In its infancy we trace a developing organization. Early on there were disciples who became apostles. As the Church progressed and was organized in various locales, the roles of elders and deacons were created. The emerging Church would through the years apply the practices and principles set forth in the canon of the sacred writings for the Church's continuance, expansion and work. In the Middle Ages clergy dominated the church, and for the most part the people were kept igno-

---

[109] See Mt. 16:19 & 18:5-18 regarding what is forbidden ("bound") and what is allowed ("loosed"), and a commentary on this in William Barclay, *The Gospel of Matthew* Vol. 2 (Philadelphia: The Westminster Press, 1975), 145-146. See also the following scriptures: Rom. 16:17, 1 Cor. 5:1-13, Gal. 5:10 & 6:1, 1 Th. 5:14, 2 Th. 3:6, 14-15, 2 Tim. 6:3-5, Tit. 1:13 & 3:10.

rant. By the time of Martin Luther and John Calvin in the 1500's, those who protested certain methods and beliefs of the dominant church, paved the way, even through personal sacrifice, for regular folks like you and me to have the scriptures available for our own reading, study and application, and in our own language.

It then became the privilege and duty of clergy to help their flocks understand the scriptures, to teach them the basic content of the Christian faith as contained in and formulated from the Bible. In many circles *catechisms* (from the Greek *catechesis*, meaning oral instruction) in the form of questions and answers were used as tools to provide instruction to prospective converts and members. In order for converts and those preparing for membership into a particular local church family to be officially received, the questions and answers had to be learned, memorized and spoken. In what historians refer to as the Ancient Church, perhaps 200 to 450 or so, learners preparing for conversion and admission into not only the invisible church but also a local congregation were called *catechumens*. The instruction was referred to as *catechetical instruction*. Brethren founder Alexander Mack Sr. (1675-1735) prepared such instruction entitled *Rites and Ordinances and Ground Searching Questions*[110] in the form of a conversation between a Father and a Son, a technique not uncommon in the early 1700's. Catechisms in written form are used today in a number of Christian denominations. Preparation for effective Christian discipleship and as members of local churches is not only appropriate, it is vital to ensure the work of Christ will be accomplished with the kind of integrity, intelligence and thoroughness which is God-honoring. Church membership classes in which the truths of the faith and the particular historical tradition are studied and appreciated are important for training in righteousness, for effective service, and for cultivating a oneness in the family of believers in that particular locale. After all, God has provided for our salvation and spiritual advancement with great detail. Jesus, our model, submitted to baptism as a sign of his acceptance of the

---

[110]Alexander Mack, Sr. *Rites & Ordinances and Ground Searching Questions* (Ashland, Ohio: The National Sunday School Association of the Brethren Church, 1939).

Father's will and plan for redemption, and he was thoroughly prepared for his ministry. We should do the same.

The Church is God's gift to the planet. We are a royal priesthood (1 Pet. 2:5 & 9), a household of faith (Eph. 2:19, 1 Pet. 2:5), God's agency on earth through which the rest of humanity may be introduced and led to follow Jesus Christ. Local churches and local church membership are the primary means for the carrying out of our responsibilities as disciples of Jesus, God's ambassadors to a world in need.

Chapter Fourteen
Rite of Holy Communion

Remembering Our Substitute Sacrifice

For approximately 2000 years Christians have enacted the actions of Jesus in the Upper Room. In some traditions the observance is called Holy *Communion* because of the fellowship we have with God through faith in Jesus, a relationship which is symbolized in the acts of eating and drinking together. In some faith communities the event is called the *Eucharist*. As mentioned above, the term is derived from the New Testament Greek word *eucharistía* which means *thanksgiving*. Jesus gave thanks (1 Cor. 11:24; see also 1 Cor. 10:16, Mt. 26:26), then broke bread and offered the cup to the disciples. Holy Communion is a ritual through which we give thanks for Jesus' sacrifice for our sins.

Sometimes the observance is referred to as a *memorial*, meaning special *remembrance*. Whenever we eat the bread and drink from the cup in this intentional way, we remember Jesus (1 Cor. 11:24-25, Lk. 22:19) whom God the Father offered on the cross, that whoever truly trusts in him, will not spiritually perish, but have eternal life, life from the eternal God both now and in the hereafter. This is the offer and the promise of God.

In some churches Holy Communion is referred to as an *ordinance* (1 Cor. 11:2 KJV) which means *authoritative orders*. Jesus specifically directed or *commanded* the disciples to do these things in remembrance of him. He said *take, eat, and drink* (Mt. 26:26-28). He said: "Do this in remembrance of me" (1 Cor. 11:24-25).

In other Christian traditions the Lord's Supper reenactment is referred to as a *sacrament*, a term from the Latin (L. *sacramentum*) meaning *consecration*. In such traditions the emphasis is placed upon the *grace of God* which we believe is imparted to believers upon their faithful observance of the actions. Because the sign-acts of breaking bread and drinking from the cup carry with them, it seems to me, both aspects of *requirement* (ordinance) and *blessing* (John 13:17, as in sacrament), it may be more helpful to simply call the experience a *rite*. As we have mentioned previously, *rites* are *ceremonies* which *sign* spiritual meaning. All rites (e.g. baptism, the Eucharist, feet-washing, the imposition of ashes in some other traditions, the anointing with oil, and laying on of hands) are intended to be outward signs of inward God-given graces. Alexander Mack Sr. wrote his explanation of these special observances as the *Rites and Ordinances* of the church.[111] It was C. F. Yoder (1873-1955) who, in his text *God's Means of Grace*,[112] explained the Brethren understanding of the full observance of the Upper Room experience (the Love Feast), with feet-washing, the small meal, and the partaking of the bread and cup, as means through which God desires to grace believers. In John 13:17, for example, Jesus said regarding the significance of feet-washing: "Now that you know these things, you will be blessed if you do them." Jesus intended that through *participation* persons will have instilled in their hearts and minds the meanings attached to the rites, thus serving to cultivate devotion and commitment.

Following his resurrection, Jesus appeared to disciples on the road to Emmaus. When they reached the village Jesus dined with them. John 24:30-31 says: "When he was at the table with them, he took bread, gave thanks, broke it and began to give it to them. Then their eyes were opened and they recognized him, and he disappeared from their sight." The rite of Holy Communion is observed to open hearts and minds to the meanings of the actions of Jesus on our behalf, to help us observe and celebrate the fellowship we share with God through faith in Jesus. The observances of the Upper Room serve as a way of remembering

---

[111]Alexander Mack, *A Short and Plain View of the Outward, Yet Sacred Rites and Ordinances of the House of God* (Mansfield, Ohio: The Century Printing Company, 1939).

[112]C. F. Yoder, *God's Means of Grace* (Elgin, Illinois: Brethren Publishing House, 1908) is the classic Brethren text on the rites of the church. See also Joseph Shultz, *The Soul of the Symbols: A Theological Study of Holy Communion* (Grand Rapids: William B. Eerdmans Publishing Company, 1966), and *The Brethren Encyclopedia* article on public worship cited previously.

Jesus' humility and his admonition to the disciples to be humble and to be concerned more for others than for self; and of remembering Jesus' sacrifice on the cross for our sins. The communion experience enables us, as a community of faith, intentionally to offer thanksgiving for all God has done in Christ to make possible our salvation; and to offer thanksgiving for the family of faith in which and through which we grow and serve as Christians. Moreover, as we do these things, each person shares in *keeping alive the proclamation* of Jesus' death for our sins. As Paul explained: "For whenever you eat this bread and drink this cup, you proclaim the Lord's death until he comes" (1 Cor. 11:26).

We see there are a number of ways to think about the observance of the Upper Room event. There are multiple meanings attached to the actions as well as the elements themselves which sign Jesus' humility, our fellowship of love with one another, and Jesus' broken body and shed blood. It is important for us to probe further, specifically the significance of what was being accomplished by God in Christ on the cross, this most important moment in time which we remember through reenactment of taking the bread and the cup; this central act of God which made possible the offer of the salvation of souls. What was God in Christ accomplishing on the cross which demands our thanks and worship? How are we to understand the crucifixion? We should say that we may never fully comprehend all that God has done for us; but the way God chose to help us understand is clear enough. We learn of the significance of Christ's death from within the Jewish tradition of sacrificial worship. So we shall go back even further in time to examine how Jesus' death is to be understood.

The Jewish Day of Atonement

Most adults have probably heard of the Jewish observance called *Yom Kippur*. It takes place annually in the fall season. *Yom* means Day; *Kippur* means Atonement, hence the English rendering of this observance. Leviticus 16 gives the details of the Day of Atonement as it was originally observed.

The overall purpose of *Yom Kippur* was to make amends; that is, to atone for the sins of the people. God instructed Moses that sacrifices were to be offered by the High Priest for his own sins and for the sins of all the people. Included in the ritual were prayers of confession, and fasting for a twenty-four hour period. It was a ceremony of renewal and cleansing, an attempt to be in fellowship with God. To be "at one" with God is to be in harmony, to be at peace with God. Only when sins are confessed and forgiven can true peace with God be accomplished. Actually, *Kippur* most literally means *covering*. The idea is that when sacrifices were offered, the sins of the people were *covered*, not to be seen by a holy God. The Israelites were well aware of the fact that all people sin, that sin separates us from God, and that something must be done to restore a harmonious relationship with God. The sacrificial system of worship was God's way of making peace possible. The people were to respond by outward observance accompanied by inner contrition and repentance.

The most impressive component of the Day of Atonement was the part having to do with the scapegoat. The high priest symbolically laid the sins of the people for the previous calendar year on the head of the scapegoat, and then the sin-laden creature was banished into the desert to perish.

What took place in that act? In it we discern God's gracious acceptance of a *substitute* offering for sin. Atonement was accomplished by the offering of a *substitute victim*. Sins were covered; the hindrances to reconciliation were banished. Understanding this, David could affirm in Psalm 32:1: "Blessed is he whose transgressions are forgiven, whose sins are covered."

The Christian Day of Atonement

With this background of understanding we are able to have more clarity regarding the *why* of our Christian communion observance. Our desire, as it was for the Hebrews, is to be in communion with God, to be at peace with God, to have our sins forgiven. The graciousness of God is his offer of Jesus as our substitute sacrifice. *Jesus* is the *substitutionary atonement* for our sins. Paul explained this to the Roman Christians: "...for all have sinned and fall short of the glory of God, and are justified freely by his grace through the redemption that came by

Christ Jesus. God presented him as a sacrifice of atonement..." (Gk. *hilasterion*, that which expiates or propitiates, Rom. 3:23-25a.).

Other Bible references which affirm again and again that Jesus is the substitute sacrifice for sins include Isaiah's prophetic words regarding the Messiah:

> ...He was pierced for our transgressions, he was crushed for our iniquities; the punishment that brought us peace was upon him, and by his wounds we are healed. We all, like sheep, have gone astray, each of us has turned to his own way; and the Lord has laid on him the iniquity of us all (Isa. 53:5-6).

Paul wrote: "Very rarely will anyone die for a righteous man, though for a good man someone might possibly dare to die. But God demonstrated his own love for us in this: While we were still sinners, Christ died for us" (Rom. 5:7). God came to *rescue* us from the grip of sin in our lives and its ultimate consequences. He came in Christ Jesus to suffer in our place, because he cares for us so much.

To the Galatians Paul wrote: "Christ redeemed us from the curse of the law by becoming a curse for us..." (Gal. 3:13). Peter wrote in his first letter: "[Christ] himself bore our sins in his body on the [cross], so that we might die to sins and live for righteousness" (1 Pet. 2:24).

God offered Jesus as the substitute bearer of our punishment. Moreover, Jesus did not have to be offered yearly as in the Jewish Day of Atonement; he was offered once for all. That's all that was needed. The writer of Hebrews explained it this way:

> ...we have been made holy through the sacrifice of Jesus Christ once for all. Day after day every priest stands and performs his religious duties; again and again he offers the same sacrifices, which can never take away sins [meaning they are simply covered]. But when this priest [Jesus] had offered for all time one sacrifice for sins, he sat down at the right hand of God (Heb. 10:10-12).

The Christian's Day of Atonement was the day Jesus was crucified in our place for our sins.

Appropriating Atonement

We may ask how are we made holy through the sacrifice of Jesus (Heb. 10:10)? Paul raised this issue when he wrote to the Corinthians. He said: "God made him who had no sin to be sin for us, so that in him we might become the righteousness of God" (2 Cor. 5:21). How may we understand our becoming righteous because of what he did? Ah, that's the point! We can do nothing to earn right standing with God. We could never be good enough. Only God could do it. Indeed, that is what he has done. He has said, in effect: "I offer you a substitute. Will you accept him? I offer you atonement. Do you want it? Jesus is the substitutionary atonement, my gift to you. Will you receive him?" We become righteous in God's sight, though not without sin, through Christ's atoning sacrifice, because our infinite, personal God has decided that that's the way it will be possible. John Calvin wrote:

> ...he assumed in a manner our place, that he might be a criminal in our [court] room, and might be dealt with as a sinner, not for his own offences, but for those of others, in as much as he was pure and exempt from every fault, and might endure the punishment that was due to us, not to himself. It is in the same manner, assuredly, that we are now righteous in him, not in respect of our rendering satisfaction to the justice of God by our own works, but because we are judged of in connection with Christ's righteousness, which we have put on by faith, that it might become ours.[113]

Clarification is needed so as not to give a false impression as to how appropriating atonement works. Jesus is the substitute sacrifice for our sins. The penalty has been paid, but for whom? For everyone? Yes, if everyone were to acknowledge Christ as their redeemer. Does everyone accept the gift of Christ as the substitutionary atonement for their sins? Unfortunately no. But for all who do, to all who believe in him, God declares righteous (John 1:12). We are holy in God's sight by our connection with Christ by faith. In the same passage quoted above in

---

[113]From John Calvin's commentary on 2 Corinthians 5:21 as given in *Calvin's Commentaries*, Volume XX (Grand Rapids: Baker Book House, 1993 reprint), 242.

which Paul said God presented Jesus as a sacrifice of atonement, he also wrote: "This righteousness from God comes through faith in Jesus Christ to all who believe" (Rom. 3:22). God "justifies those who have faith in Jesus (v. 26; see also Phil. 3:8-9, and Eph. 3:12). That's how people are forgiven of their sins, by their repentance, thanksgiving, and faith in Jesus. *The offer of Jesus as a substitute sacrifice for our sins is what we commemorate in the sharing of the bread and the cup.* Of course, it is not only for us to ceremonially remember Jesus' love actions, it is necessary for us to respond internally by our faith and commitment to him as well.

Throughout history royal families have received special treatment. Often they were exempt from keeping the law or receiving punishment or even discipline. Royal children still needed to know, however, that when they misbehaved, they deserved to be punished. It is known that when a prince or princess disobeyed or did poorly in schoolwork, the punishment was given to a *whipping boy*, as he was called, instead. There was no doubt who was really at fault, but it was simply unthinkable in some traditions for a royal child to be spanked.[114]

On the human level, that was a rather cruel and arrogant practice. On the spiritual level, we may say it is the love of God which permitted Jesus to be the whipping boy for us. He was offered to receive the eternal punishment we deserve. When we receive the elements of Holy Communion, let us be keenly aware and thankful that what we are remembering and proclaiming is the atonement for sins God offers us through faith in Jesus Christ. He is our substitute sacrifice.

Administration

While there are some variations in the manners of conducting the Love Feast, the primary elements and setting are common in Brethren congregations. The parish I've served in Burlington observes the Love Feast on the first Sundays of October (World Communion Sunday) and January (as a start to the New Year), and on Maundy Thursday (the observance of the Upper Room). Each service is held in the evening

---

[114]Adapted from *Our Daily Bread* (Grand Rapids: RBC Ministries, Volume 38, Number 10, January 8, 1994).

with candle-lighted tables. From the sample service given below, it is observed that there are five sections to the order, which may extend an hour or more.

Whereas Paul encouraged the Corinthian Christians to examine themselves before partaking of the elements of the bread and the cup, so the service begins with a time of *preparation*. The second section is where all are invited to exemplify and cultivate the humble, servant heart by engaging in *feet-washing*. The administration of this will be addressed at the close of the next chapter. The third component is the sharing of a small symbolic *meal*, remembering the setting of the observance in the Upper Room. In the fourth section of the service, all participate in the *Eucharist*, taking the bread and the cup in thanksgiving and remembrance of Jesus' shed blood and broken body.

Throughout the service, the deacons serve as readers of the various scriptures and offer the prayers. The pastor provides introductory, explanatory remarks for each section. The service concludes with the quoting of Mark 14:26 followed by the *singing of a hymn* and *departing quietly*.

Rite of Holy Communion

The Love Feast

PREPARATION

Welcome & Introductory Remarks

Hymn "Hallelujah, What a Savior" (Stanzas 1-4)

Reading 1 Corinthians 11:27-34

Moments of Silent Confession & The Lord's Prayer

ORDINANCE OF SERVING LOVE

Preparatory Remarks

Reading   John 13:1-5, 12-17

Hymn "I Have Decided to Follow Jesus"

Feet-washing

(Hymns may be sung during this time by those waiting.)

ORDINANCE OF SHARING LOVE

Preparatory Remarks

Reading   John 13:33-35

Hymn "They'll Know We Are Christians by Our Love" (Stanzas 1, 2, 3)

Prayer of Blessing

The Agape Meal

(The sharing of testimonies is welcomed during the meal.)

ORDINANCE OF REDEEMING LOVE

Words of Institution Mark 14:22-25

Hymn "Let Us Break Bread Together" (Stanzas 1, 2)

Prayer of Consecration for the Bread

Partaking of the Bread (All):

WE BREAK THIS BREAD AS A SIGN
OF JESUS' BODY BROKEN FOR US.

Prayer of Consecration for the Cup

Partaking of the Cup (All):

WE DRINK THIS CUP AS A SIGN
OF JESUS' BLOOD SHED FOR OUR SINS.

Moments of Silence

CLASSIC WORSHIP

Prayer of Thanksgiving (All):
GRACIOUS GOD, WE THANK YOU FOR THE EXAMPLE OF JESUS, HIS SACRIFICE FOR OUR SINS, FOR THE LOVE OF THE BRETHREN, AND FOR ENABLING US TO BE PARTAKERS OF THESE MEMORIALS. BLESS US, WE PRAY, FOR CONTINUED AND FRUITFUL SERVICE TO YOU AND THOSE AROUND US: THROUGH JESUS CHRIST OUR LORD. AMEN.

DISMISSAL BENEDICTION

Mark 14:26

Hymn "Blest Be the Tie"

Blest be the tie that binds
Our hearts in Christian love.
The fellowship of kindred minds
Is like to that above.

(Please depart quietly.)

Chapter Fifteen

Rite of Feet-washing

Servant-hood Symbolized

In contemporary church life feet-washing is not practiced regularly by most communities of faith, although the Roman church restored it in its Holy Week rituals in 1956, and other churches are rediscovering the practice. It may be fair to assume that the thought of doing such a thing in public in our Western culture lacks good taste. And yet, there remain a few Christian bodies which retain the rite and do so, first, because they adhere to the authority of scripture; secondly, therefore, as given in John 13, they believe Jesus commanded the practice (13:14) as well as what it symbolized: "you also should wash one another's feet;" thirdly, because Jesus gave his disciples a powerful example in this action, and a powerful action which carries with it a life-style significance and application (13:15): "I have set you an example that you should do as I have done for you;" and fourthly, because Jesus promised a blessing for those who do it (13:17): "Now that you know these things, you will be blessed if you do them." The Brethren Church is one of the denominations which includes the practice of feet-washing in its Service of Holy Communion because the action carries with it a significance nowhere else provided for, liturgically speaking, in the corporate assembly, and which we believe should be portrayed and enacted so that what it symbolizes may be instilled and engrained in our minds and hearts, and then hopefully applied in daily life. Presently we will examine the passage in John's Gospel which gives the account of Jesus' washing the disciples' feet as the authority for the practice. We will describe the context, that is, the setting of this Upper Room sign-act of Jesus; we shall note the purpose of the action, and then give interpretation and application.

Setting and Purpose

Just prior to this event, as given in John 12, Jesus had made his triumphal entry into Jerusalem. It was the beginning of the end of his ministry, the culmination, the climax, the apex, the time when everything was coming to a head and a conclusion. The crowds were there in Jerusalem for the Passover Feast. They took palm branches, laid some on the road as a sign of welcoming a king. They shouted "Hosanna," which means *save us*. "Blessed is he who comes in the name of the Lord." The Pharisees and others were stirred up against him. Before the fateful betrayal and the final acts would unfold, Jesus gathered the disciples to share a last meal, give them special words of instruction, and present them with special examples in the feet-washing and the partaking of the bread and the cup.

The immediate setting is given in John 13:1-2: "It was just before the Passover Feast...The evening meal was being served, and the devil had already prompted Judas Iscariot, son of Simon, to betray Jesus." The specific purpose for the gathering is given in 13:1 & 3: "Jesus knew that the time had come for him to leave this world and go to the Father...[He] knew that the Father had put all things under his power, and that he had come from God [the Father] and was returning to [him]...Having loved his own who were in the world, he now showed them the full extent of his love..."

Jesus' forthcoming action not only was going to demonstrate the extent of his love, it would sign as well the disciples' responsibility as imitators and ambassadors of the Savior. The sign-action is given in verses 4 & 5. "So he got up from the meal, took off his outer clothing, and wrapped a towel around his waste. After that, he poured water into a basin and began to wash his disciples' feet, drying them with the towel that was wrapped around him." We may ask: How or why was this action of feet-washing a demonstration of the full extent of his love? The explanation is given through Jesus' subsequent dialogue with Peter.

Interpretation

Peter was confused. Of course he was not the only one to miss the points of so many of Jesus' teachings and actions. As given in the

Rite of Feet-washing

Gospel of John and elsewhere, Jesus would often communicate the heavenly, the spiritual, in terms of the familiar, the tangible. That was his intent with the washing of the disciples' feet, that which a servant would perform for those entering a household. On this occasion there would not have been a servant to perform the act when they arrived. Utilizing the opportunity to make a point, Jesus played the familiar role of a slave to portray, enact, demonstrate, emphasize and teach that not only was he going to actually, spiritually, take that role in the offering of himself for the sins of humanity, but also that they as his imitators and ambassadors must assume a servant posture in life before others in their relating and witnessing. Confused Peter asked Jesus why he was doing this, how could he or would he wash their feet?

There is much to Jesus' response, more than simply a reply to the immediate question. To understand Jesus' reply we must refer to the Gospel of Luke. You will recall in that account of the Last Supper, that "a dispute arose among them as to which of them was considered to be the greatest" (Lk. 22:24). Here Jesus was shortly to be offering himself through crucifixion, and the disciples were arguing over prestige! Jesus could have become bitter and angry. Instead he took the opportunity to demonstrate the full extent of his love. However, he also taught them something more related to their arguing.

There is no doubt that in Jesus' reply there is an allusion to baptism and its significance. Verse 8 says: "Unless I wash you, you have no part with me." In other words, Jesus began his response by offering a deeper meaning. In effect he said: "Unless you experience a profession of faith and are baptized, you will have no station in the kingdom of God." Peter responded again on the level of surface meaning, for it was unthinkable for a Rabbi to wash his disciples' feet, but rather the other way around was a possibility. Peter replied: "not just my feet but my hands and my head as well!" (v.9) "Jesus answered, 'A person who has had a bath needs only to wash his feet; his whole body is clean. And you are clean, though not every one of you.' For he knew who was going to betray him..." (vv. 10-11). What is meant by this exchange?

William Barclay (1907-1978) explained: "It was the custom that before people went to a feast they bathed themselves. When they came to the house of their host, they did not need to be bathed again; all they needed was to have their feet washed. The washing of the feet was the ceremony which preceded entry into the house where they were to be guests..."[115] In similar thinking, Jesus said to Peter, therefore, and with deeper significance: "It is not the bathing of your body that you require. That you can do for yourself. What you need is the washing which marks entry into the household of faith."[116] As Jesus used it, the bath symbolized the washing of regeneration. Baptism, which carries with it a profession of faith, signs a submission of one's will to the will of God the Father. So what was Jesus saying, especially in light of the dispute over greatness? If anyone is too proud to submit to the washing rite of entry into the household of faith, then it is his pride which shuts him out of the kingdom.[117] That is one dimension of meaning in this dialogue. Submission to the washing of entry, signified by baptism, is essential.

Secondly, following that humbling of self before God, there must be a continuation of that kind of attitude and action when relating to others. Jesus said: "I have set an example that you should do as I have done for you...no servant is greater than his master, nor is a messenger greater than the one who sent him" (vv. 15-16). Jesus was submitting to the will of the Father. Feet-washing was a tangible way to focus on that submission and servant nature which he was and would exemplify on the cross, and which all disciples should embrace and exemplify in their day-to-day living.

We gain an even greater appreciation for Jesus' demonstration as we ponder the description Paul formulated or quoted in his letter to the Philippians.

> Do nothing out of selfish ambition or vain conceit, but in humility consider others better than yourselves. Each of you should look not only to your own interests, but also to the

---

[115] William Barclay, *The Gospel of John* Vol. 2, rev. ed. (Philadelphia: The Westminster Press, 1975), 141.

[116] Ibid.

[117] Ibid., 142.

Rite of Feet-washing

interests of others. Your attitude should be the same as that of Christ Jesus: Who, being in very nature God, did not consider equality with God [the Father] something to be [held on to], but made himself nothing, taking the very nature of a servant, being made in human likeness. And being found in appearance as a man, he humbled himself and became obedient to death-- even death on a cross (Phil. 2:3-8).

So the full extent of Jesus' love displayed through feet-washing, included his willingness to take the form, the role of a servant, to set aside greatness, to humble himself for the sake of others, to submit to the will of the Father, to offer himself for the redemption of souls. He was willing to do what a slave would do. He was willing to cast aside pride, position and status, and not think of himself more highly that anyone should. He set an example for all disciples, which they and we should do as he had done.

Application

Barclay has given words of application which are without compare.

Here is the lesson that there is only one kind of greatness, the greatness of service. The world is full of people who are standing on their [pride] when they ought to be kneeling at the feet of their brethren. In every sphere of life desire for prominence and unwillingness to take a subordinate place wreck the scheme of things. [An athlete] is one day omitted from the team and refuses to play anymore. An aspiring politician is passed over for some office to which he thought he had a right and refuses to accept any subordinate office. A member of a choir is not given a solo and will not sing any more. In any [group] it may happen that someone is given a quite unintentional slight and either explodes in anger or broods [and sulks] for days afterwards. When we are tempted to think of our dignity, our prestige, our rights, let us see again the picture of the Son of God, [wrapped] with a towel, kneeling at his disciples' feet.[118]

---

[118]Ibid., 139-140.

All of the above are why the Brethren have placed such a high value on the practice of feet-washing. Whereas baptism signs our identification with the death and resurrection of Jesus, our dying to self and rising to newness of life, and therefore, our entry into the kingdom of God's grace; and whereas in Holy Communion, the Eucharist, we remember the shed blood and broken body of our Lord, his sacrifice; in feet-washing, unlike anywhere else in scripture, the point is made so vividly of our identification with and our responsibility to copy, pattern, and exemplify the servant nature of our humble Savior. Moreover, since feet-washing is done on behalf of another, so also we are moved to do for others in daily life that which will be to their benefit.[119]

A hymn included in the hymnal of the Old German Baptist Brethren interprets and celebrates the rite.

> Jesus his garments laid aside,
> And wash'd his servants' feet,
> To teach that neither scorn nor pride
> For us is right and meet.
>
> And when our "Lord and Master" thus
> Did condescend, he too
> A plain commandment gave to us,
> That we the same should do.
>
> Then, when we thus together meet,
> To hold a feast of love,
> We'll stoop and wash each other's feet,
> And our obedience prove.

---

[119] It seems to me, therefore, that the weight of meaning in John 13 may be on what feet-washing symbolizes rather than on the action itself, and may be viewed as debatable regarding its obligatory sacramental practice within the corporate assembly. One reason is the lack of further comment on the subject in any of Paul's letters, whereas baptism and the Lord's Table are referenced. However, it also seems, if we desire to embrace the scriptures and our Lord's teachings and example in all their fullness, the practice of feet-washing within the observance of the Upper Room event should be highly valued, graciously encouraged and included without apology, for our lives as Christians are admonished to be characterized by servant-hood. Nowhere else has Jesus given us such a powerful and ongoing vehicle for instilling this quality in our minds and hearts.

Rite of Feet-washing

Lord, to thy holy word we go,
Thy promise there we plead,
That those who practice what they know
Shall happy be, indeed.

Dear Savior, wash our souls, we pray,
In the blest fountain pure,
And give us strength, that we ne'er stray,
But to the end endure.[120]

Administration

In our congregation for the feet-washing component of the Love Feast, men and women depart to separate rooms where they pair with one another. One person sits down while the other wraps a long towel around his/her waist, then kneels down before the other, a basin of water placed on the floor. The person sitting, having taken off his shoes and foot garments, places one foot in the basin, whereupon the partner cups some water and pours it over the other's foot. After drying the foot with the towel, the other foot is placed in the basin to be symbolically washed similarly. The persons switch places, the towel is transferred as well, and the second person's feet are washed. Upon completion of both, they may offer one another an embrace with an expression of Christian love. Some may even offer what the Bible refers to as a *holy kiss* (2 Pet. 5:14). Either one of these gestures are traditional Brethren practices at the close of the feet-washing ritual.[121]

---

[120] Hymn 312 in *A Collection of Hymns and Sacred Songs of the Brethren of the Old German Baptist Church*, Twelfth Edition (Ashland, Ohio: Garber Publishing and MFG Co., 1927).

[121] *The Brethren Encyclopedia Volume* 2, 1378.

Chapter Sixteen

Rite of Anointing

The Lord's Day, above all days in each week, is set aside for worship and rest from the regular routine and responsibilities of the other days, not only because God deserves it and we need it, but also because God commands it. "Six days you shall labor and do all your work, but the seventh day is a Sabbath to the Lord your God..." (Ex. 20:9-10). The day of resurrection of Jesus was a kind of Sabbath as well, in that it was on that day that the eternal rest we have by faith in him was made possible in this life and foreshadowed for the rest of eternity.

The regular weekly worship event is one of the ways God has provided for our being refreshed, sustained, strengthened, built-up in faith, and equipped for the rest of our spiritual journey. Whereas baptism and confirmation mark the beginning of our walk with God, various other means of God's grace are available to us to carry us along on our pilgrimage,[122] including weekly worship, private prayer, the absorption and application of the scriptures, and the ordinances of the Lord's Supper and anointing with oil.[123]

Not only did Jesus, the night he was betrayed, institute the taking of the bread and the cup, and demonstrate cleansing from sin and servant love in the action of feet-washing (Mt. 26:26-28, Mk. 14:17-21, Lk. 22:14-18, Jn. 13:1-12, 1 Cor. 11:24-26), after his resurrection, on the first day of the week, following his teaching the scriptures to disciples on the road, it was at his sharing of the bread and the cup with them which enabled their minds and eyes to recognize who he was (Lk. 24:13-32). It is this pattern of communicating the scriptures followed by the sharing of the bread and the cup which has informed and continues to shape weekly worship orders worldwide. Corporate worship,

---

[122]Jerry R. Flora, *The Message of Faith: An Exposition on the First Half of 'A Centennial Statement'* (Ashland, Ohio: The Brethren Church, Inc., 1996), 123. In the present treatment of the rite of anointing we are drawing substantially from Dr. Flora's work.

[123]Ibid.

including the preaching of the word of God, the singing of the faith, and the observance of the upper room experience, are some of the means of grace God has provided for carrying along believers on our spiritual walk with God.

One of the means of God's grace[124] less spoken of generally, and which is a distinctive inclusion in Brethren church rites, is anointing with oil. Most often this rite is administered in the privacy of one's home or in the hospital, the purpose being primarily to help persons who are facing difficult circumstances, particularly any type of illness, whether physical infirmity or emotional stress or disorder. What follows is an explanation of the significance of the *Rite of Anointing*, one of God's means of grace.

Anointing in Scripture

Anointing, a term which means to apply oil or ointment, has a long history of uses in the biblical record, and which demonstrates its employment for various purposes and situations. For example, anointing was carried out for setting apart persons for special service, as in the *ordination* of Aaron and his sons to the priesthood. This elaborate ritual is described in Exodus 29:1-9, of which verse seven says: "Take the anointing oil and anoint him by pouring it on his head." In Exodus 40 is described the anointing of the Tabernacle and its furnishings, as well as Aaron that he may be *consecrated* to serve as priest.

The anointing of Saul as king is described in 1 Samuel 10. Verse 1 reads: "Then Samuel took a flask of oil and poured it on Saul's head and kissed him, saying, 'Has not the Lord anointed you leader over his inheritance?'" Similarly, in 1 Samuel 16:13 we find Samuel anointing David. "So Samuel took the horn of oil and anointed [David] in the presence of his brothers, and from that day on the Spirit of the Lord came upon David in power..."

Of course we are familiar with Jesus' baptism at which he was anointed by the Holy Spirit that he may begin and carry out his ministry (Mt. 3:16-17). To that event Jesus spoke when he was in the syn-

---

[124]The description of the rites and ceremonies of the church as means of God's grace is the distinctive theme of C. F. Yoder's *God's Means of Grace*.

Rite of Anointing

agogue in Nazareth. He cited Isaiah 61:1-2: "The Spirit of the Lord is on me, because he has anointed me to preach good news to the poor..." (Lk. 4:18-19; see also Acts 10:36-38). In this regard I would call to our remembrance that *Messiah* in Hebrew and *Christ* in Greek, both designations of Jesus' role, mean *the anointed one*. Moreover, not only was Jesus anointed at the beginning of his ministry, but also at the close. You will recall the account given in Matthew 26:6-13 which speaks of a woman pouring expensive perfume on Jesus' head. All of the above are illustrations of being anointed for calling to special service.

The second major purpose of anointing as given in scripture is for health concerns. God has called us to advance his kingdom and do his will. He has not left us without the strength and the resources, our daily bread, not the least of which is good health, to accomplish his purposes. I mention this because God cares about our whole being, our bodies, minds and emotions. The same God who created the universe cares for us in our needs and wants to equip us for the doing of his will.

In scriptural accounts we discover various means used for healings. For example in 2 Kings 5:14 we read of Naaman who "dipped himself in the Jordan seven times, as the man of God had told him, and his flesh was restored and became clean like that of a young boy." Isaiah 38:21 describes the healing of Hezekiah: "prepare a poultice [meaning a warm, moistened mass] of figs and apply it to the boil, and he will recover." Mark 6:12-13 describes the ministry of the Twelve who were sent out by Jesus. "They went out and preached that people should repent. They drove out many demons and anointed many sick people with oil and healed them." And the account of Jesus healing a man born blind says he used saliva and mud as the means of healing (Jn. 9:6-7).

From 1 Corinthians 12:9, 28, 30 we remember the early church recognized gifts of healing, which suggests a variety of approaches were and are possible, including medical care and direct divine intervention.[125] "As witness to the use of human learning and skill, Paul included among his most trusted companions the physician Luke (Col. 4:14)."[126] "Oils of various kinds were widely employed for medical purposes in the biblical world (Luke 10:34). Oil could also represent

---

[125]Flora, 136-137.

[126]Ibid., 137.

the presence and power of the Spirit of God. In the wilderness tabernacle, for example, an 'eternal flame' of pure olive oil burned continuously (Ex. 27:20)."[127]

The practice of anointing given by Jesus to the Twelve was carried on by the early church, as given in James 5:13-16:

> Is any one of you in trouble? He should pray. Is anyone happy? Let him sing songs of praise. Is any one of you sick? He should call the elders of the church to pray over him and anoint him with oil in the name of the Lord. And the prayer offered in faith will make the sick person well; the Lord will raise him up. If he has sinned, he will be forgiven. Therefore confess your sins to each other and pray for each other so that you may be healed. The prayer of a righteous man is powerful and effective.

Jerry Flora has commented: "The emphasis in James is on confession, prayer, and the willing power of God to act on our behalf...We can believe that healing is God's primary will for believers and pray with that in mind. The infinite Spirit, however, is never under our control or subject to our manipulation. Scripture reports cases of unhealed illness which must in some way fall within the will of God: Elisha, who healed many, fell sick and died (2 Kings 13:14); Paul, who healed many, had an incurable 'thorn in the flesh' (2 Cor. 12:7-9); Epaphroditus, who ministered to Paul, nearly died from an illness which the apostle did not--or could not--cure (Phil. 2:27, 30); and Trophimus, one of Paul's traveling companions, was so sick he had to be left behind (2 Tim. 4:20)...We can draw several inferences from this. First, God chooses not to heal some illness, either by medicine or miracle. God's ways are beyond us as the heavens are above the earth (Isa. 55:9), and sometimes we must believe that death itself is the final healing for those who are children of eternity. Therefore, unhealed sickness need not indicate lack of faith, and those not cured must not be so reprimanded. Second, some illness is caused by sin (Mk. 2:5-10; Jn. 5:14), but not all (Jn. 9:1-3)."[128]

---

[127]Ibid.

[128]Ibid., 138.

Rite of Anointing

For example, evidently the sins of the paralytic spoken of in Mark 2:5-10 had at least in part caused his condition. Jesus said to him: "Son, your sins are forgiven...get up, take your mat and go home" (from Mk. 2:5 & 11). And to the invalid mentioned in John 5, the one who had been seeking healing at a pool, Jesus declared: "Stop sinning or something worse may happen to you." Some illnesses are caused by sin, as with Aids. However, in the case of the man born blind, given in John 9, the disciples asked Jesus: "'Rabbi, who sinned, this man or his parents, that he was born blind?' 'Neither this man nor his parents sinned,' said Jesus, 'but this happened so that the work of God might be displayed in his life'" (Jn. 9:2-3). Lack of healing, therefore, does not mean there was a specific sin cause, and those who remain unhealed must not be criticized by other Christians.[129] On the other hand, we should understand that all illness really has its root in the sin of the fall, as told in Genesis. Nevertheless, to attribute a disease of a particular person to some sin in their life is an unwarranted judgment. Only God knows the source or the reason.

However, when sin is present in a person's life, which may cause emotional stress, and may even take its toll in physical collapse, repentance and confession would be the beginning of the healing process. Psalm 32 makes the point.

> When I kept silent my bones wasted away through my groaning all day long. For day and night your hand was heavy upon me; my strength was sapped as in the heat of summer. Then I acknowledged my sin to you and did not cover up my iniquity. I said, "I will confess my transgressions to the Lord"--and you forgave the guilt of my sin. (Ps. 32:4-5)

Praying with anointing is a biblical way to enable the healing process to begin. This leads us to the inclusion in James, a testimony of the early church's value placed on this intentional action with regard to health concerns. The elders of the church may be called to pray over individuals and anoint them with oil in the name of the Lord. If they have sinned, they will be forgiven. Therefore, individuals should con-

---

[129] Ibid.

fess their sins that they may be healed. We may understand that while prayers may be offered for healing, they are offered also to help persons cope with their circumstances, should God's will be that they must endure their conditions. In either case, prayer with anointing with oil is a blessed rite of the church. The availability and employment of this should periodically be explained and graciously offered.

Administration

In the administration of the rite in Brethren churches, deacons and the pastor gather with those desiring anointing and prayer. The scriptural basis for the rite (Ja. 5:13-16) is read and explained. Then all are given opportunity to confess their sins silently to God. The pastor then places some oil making the sign of the cross on the person's forehead, followed by the deacons and the pastor laying hands and praying for the healing and care of the individual. In so doing the person anointed will have placed his/her life in the hands and purpose of the Great Physician, whether it be for literal divine healing, strength for forthcoming medical attention, spiritual and emotional inner peace, any and all of the above, and assurance of the future resurrection.

In the hymnal of the Old German Baptist Church are hymns which emphasize the special-ness of the *Rite of Anointing*. Two excerpts are given here.

> When struggling on the bed of pain,
> And earth and all its joys are vain,
> How sweet, my God, to know thy pow'r
> Sustains me in this trying hour.
>
> I call the elders here, O Lord,
> To do according to thy word;
> And while the oil's by faith applied,
> Oh, may my soul be sanctified.[130]
>
> Great God, be pleased to hear us now,
> While we to thee would humbly bow;

---

[130] *A Collection of Hymns and Sacred Songs of the Brethren of the Old German Baptist Church*, from Hymn 320.

In mercy now the sick do view,
Who're still disposed thy will to do.

May they now be abundant blest;
Restore them if thou seest best;
If not, may they endeavor still,
To be submissive to thy will.

May they be thy Spirit led,
While we the oil pour on their head;
This duty from thy word we claim,
T'anoint the sick in thy blest name.[131]

Whether it be triune immersion baptism, three-fold communion, or anointing with oil, ours in The Brethren Church is a rich heritage of practicing that which God has made available in the classic rites and ceremonies of the church, for in the faithful participation of them, God imparts his grace for believing, for growing in faith, for carrying us along on our spiritual pilgrimage. We should be ever thankful.

---

[131] Ibid., from Hymn 322.

Chapter Seventeen
The Spiritual Discipline of Fasting

When you fast, do not look somber as the hypocrites do, for they disfigure their faces to show men they are fasting. I tell you the truth, they have received their reward in full. But when you fast, put oil on your head and wash your face, so that it will not be obvious to men that you are fasting, but only to your Father, who is unseen; and your Father, who sees what is done in secret, will reward you (Mt. 6:16-18).

Some of the practices in which we as Christians engage may be labeled *spiritual disciplines*. A spiritual discipline is a practice which helps us grow in Christ and stay on the right spiritual course, both individually and by extension as a collective Body of believers. Examples of spiritual disciplines are praying, worshiping, studying the scriptures, and tithing. Lesser known or practiced in many Christian circles is *fasting*. Fasting was discussed by Jesus within what we refer to as the Sermon on the Mount (Matthew 5-7), as given above.

We are including a discussion of fasting because in The Brethren Church, as demonstrated previously, there is intentionality about doing those *rituals* which our Lord authorized and exemplified as means of God imparting his grace to the faithful and obedient believer. While fasting may not be viewed in the same classification with baptism or the Lord's Supper, and may not be thought of as a ritual as such for rituals are public sign-actions, nevertheless it is an action in which persons engage as a devotional, that is a personal and private spiritual experience of self-sacrifice and worship. We might say *fasting* is one of the *classic means of private worship*, devotion which specifically and intentionally enables believers to focus more of their attention Godward, and less of their attention on themselves. So we may say fasting is a sacred act which carries with it significant spiritual meaning. That is ritualistic, it seems to me. It is a *living ritual*, and is in harmony with the The Brethren Church's incorporation of what may be described as higher and more liturgically *involved* patterns of ceremonial expression, more than most evangelical communions of faith. Also, since praying usually accompanies the time of fasting, fasting is truly an act of personal worship and therefore suitable for inclusion in a volume of classic, biblically time-honored expressions of worshiping. Before discussing fasting more in detail, let's examine the context within which Jesus' remarks were made.

Context

Because in the Luke version of the Sermon on the Mount (Lk. 6:20-49) the 'sermon' follows the calling of the disciples, it has been referred to as a kind of ordination address. From the Matthew account, however, it becomes clearer that this passage is not a sermon at all, but rather a collection of the primary sayings of Jesus. It has been called a "brief summary of the doctrines of Jesus."[132] In other words, if one were to search for the core of Jesus' thought and instruction, the Sermon on the Mount would be the material to examine.

Included in this collection of his sayings are the well-known Beatitudes, those statements which refer to the blessedness of those who exemplify Godly characteristics (e.g. "Blessed are the poor in spirit, for there's is the kingdom of heaven" Mt. 5:3). Also included are the Similitudes ("You are the salt of the earth...You are the light of the world..." Mt. 5:13-16). The Golden Rule (Mt. 7:12) is found as well in this special section of the Bible ("So in everything, do to others what you would have them do to you...").

It was Martin Luther who said that in the Sermon on the Mount Jesus wanted to expose and oppose all false teaching and provide the true meaning of the scriptures.[133] This becomes very evident in Matthew 6, in which Jesus discussed the importance to the Jew of per-

---

[132] John Calvin, "Commentary and Harmony of the Evangelists," *Calvin's Commentaries* Vol. XVI (Grand Rapids: Baker Book House, 1993), 259.

[133] Martin Luther, "The Sermon on the Mount: Sermons," *Luther's Works* Vol. 21, Jaroslav Pelikan, ed. (St. Louis: Concordia Publishing House, 1956), 3.

forming *three essential acts of righteousness*. We might refer to them as *three spiritual disciplines: almsgiving* (giving to the needy, 6:2-4), *praying* (6:5-15), and *fasting* (6:16-18). Jesus instructed the disciples not to go about doing these things in the way "the hypocrites do in the synagogues and on the streets" (6:2), an obvious criticism of the Pharisees who took great pleasure, it seemed, in announcing their deeds. In other words, they were spiritual show-offs!

What is given in Matthew 6 then is a discourse on having the proper motive for one's acts of righteousness. Practicing piety should not be thought of as mere outward performance, because such expression can come from an ungodly motive as well as a God-honoring intention. The necessity of a "purity of intention," as John Wesley put it, is the main point Jesus was making.[134]

Regarding *almsgiving*, Jesus said, "do not announce it with trumpets, as the hypocrites do in the synagogues and on the streets." He instructed the disciples to do this act of righteousness in a quiet and inconspicuous fashion. In other words, we don't need to tell everyone what we did. God knows, the needy one knows, and we know. That's all that matters. That way it helps us keep our acts of righteousness truly righteous, rather than ostentatious.

Similarly, Jesus said that *praying* did not have to be done as a vehicle for public display, for one's focus then would not be totally Godward, but rather is interfered with or distracted by one's awareness that others are observing and hearing, and, therefore, not truly and sincerely offered. Jesus also said, do not keep "babbling like pagans," who think because they say a lot, they will be heard, and somehow will be more righteous for doing so. Jesus said one's personal prayer life should be just that, personally and privately offered.

Fasting

The third act of righteousness of which Jesus spoke was *fasting*. He assumed fasting to be one of the three essential devotional disciplines.

---

[134]John Wesley. "Upon Our Lord's Sermon on the Mount," Sermon XXVI, Discourse VI, *The Works of John Wesley*, third edition, Vol. V (Grand Rapids: Baker Book House, 1991), 328.

The New Testament term translated *fast* (Gk. *nesteuo*) means to *abstain*. The Old Testament Hebrew word (*sum*) means to cover the mouth. Thus fasting is abstaining from eating. And in the period in which one fasts, the intention is to spend more time deliberately focusing on God, while denying oneself food for a relatively brief period of time. Of course the tendency for some, at least according to Jesus' remarks about the Pharisees, was to show off their act of so-called righteousness by letting everyone know how they were suffering physically, mercifully sacrificing for God! Jesus said, when fasting make yourself look as regular and normal as you always do. Maintain your regular appearance so that no one would ever know what you were doing, and so do it as an act of devotion to God. The "purity of intention," the right motive is what Jesus was emphasizing. Needless to say, Jesus was not saying almsgiving, praying and fasting were wrong; he assumed all three were special and important spiritual disciplines. His point was that there is a right way and a poor way of doing one's acts of righteousness.

Most Christians do kindly deeds for others, and they pray. Fasting, however, at least in my church life experience for most of my formative and young adult years, generally had not been promoted or observed on any regular basis. Nor have I ever heard a sermon on the subject. And yet, the Bible teaches that this kind of short-term abstinence from food is a way we may intentionally put ourselves, individually and collectively into a reflective and prayerful spiritual posture so as to become more aware of what God may do in and through us. Fasting is a demonstration of one's willingness to seek God's help, God's direction. It may be a way people might show forth their sincerity of repentance for sins.

In Jesus' day Jews were in the habit of observing an annual fast on the Day of Atonement, the day on which since the days of Moses and Aaron, the priest would offer sacrifices for the sins of the people. In Acts 27:9 it is specifically referred to as *the Fast*. Acts 27 tells of Paul sailing for Rome. "...When the wind did not allow us to hold our course, we sailed to the lee of Crete...We moved along the coast with difficulty and came to a place called Fair Havens...Much time had been lost, and sailing had already become dangerous because by now it was after the Fast" (from Acts 27:7-9). What did he mean by this reference to the Fast? The *NIV*

Study Bible gives fine commentary. "The Jewish Day of Atonement fell in the latter part of September or in October. The usual sailing season by Jewish calculation lasted from Pentecost (May-June) to Tabernacles, which was five days after the Fast. The Romans considered sailing after September 15 doubtful and after November 11 suicidal."[135] The point for us is that there was an annual fast during this time, referred to as *the Fast* which all Jews would observe.

Beyond the annual fast, many Jews in the New Testament period also observed weekly fasts, alluded to in Luke 18 where Jesus told a parable about righteousness.

> Two men went up to the Temple to pray, one a Pharisee and the other a tax collector. The Pharisee stood up and prayed about himself: "God, I thank you that I am not like other men--robbers, evildoers, adulterers--or even like this tax collector. I fast twice a week and give a tenth of all I get." But the tax collector stood at a distance. He would not even look up to heaven, but beat his breast and said, "God, have mercy on me, a sinner." I tell you that this man, rather than the other, went home justified before God. For everyone who exalts himself will be humbled, and he who humbles himself will be exalted" (Lk. 18:10-18).

The parable's message compliments what we've already reviewed from Jesus' words about the right motive in doing acts of righteousness. We learn from the parable, confirmed by other historical accounts, that Jews observed weekly fasts on the second and fifth days of the week. These fasts were so observed because they believed Moses ascended Mount Sinai for the second tables of the Law on a Thursday and returned on a Monday. Later, in the developing church, Christians appointed Wednesdays and Fridays as days of fasting in commemoration of the passion and crucifixion of Jesus.[136]

Although Jesus rebuked the Pharisees for their poor attitude and display, he affirmed the practice, for he fasted and valued it as a spiritual

---

[135] *Zondervan NIV Study Bible* Fully Revised (Grand Rapids: Zondervan, 2002), 2308.

[136] Merrill F. Unger, *Unger's Bible Dictionary* (Chicago: Moody Press, 1957), 346.

discipline. As we know, for example, when Jesus was led by the Spirit in the desert before the commencement of his ministry, Matthew 4:2 tells us he fasted forty days and forty nights. It was an act of righteousness, a spiritual discipline, which helped him submit to the will of the Father, to be prepared for the future, and to acquire the inner strength to combat evil and the Evil One.

There are many instances of fasting mentioned in the Bible, a complete listing of which could be surveyed. Suffice it to say, in the New Testament we know of the devout prophetess Anna who met Joseph and Mary and the infant Jesus at the Temple. Luke 2:37 says: "She never left the temple but worshiped night and day, fasting and praying" (see also Mt. 17:21 in the NLT for note). And in Acts 14:21-23 we learn that Paul and Barnabas appointed elders in Lystra, Iconium and Antioch. It says, "with prayer and fasting" they committed them to the Lord. From these citations we realize that fasting was usually accompanied by praying. They went hand in hand as spiritual practices. While our Lord has not commanded that we fast, and evidently he and the disciples were not legalistic about this (e.g. Mt. 9:14, Mk. 2:18, Lk. 5:33), nevertheless he affirmed the practice by his remarks and example, especially in significant moments in time and circumstances.

Fasting is a symbol and a demonstration of one's willingness to deny self and seek God. It puts us in a position of being especially aware of our dependence upon God and especially receptive to what God may desire to communicate through his word, inner conviction of the heart, and through mental reflection. Fasting frees us from self-centeredness for a season, that we may be truly God-centered and other's-minded. And I believe, as a congregation engages in this as a collective act of devotion, God will most likely impart added insight and direction we might otherwise not have received or known. Fasting is a spiritual discipline worthy of all Christians' consideration, both individually and together intentionally as local churches. It is a classic, time-honored, biblical discipline in which, along with the rites and ceremonies of the Church, God's grace is imparted to believers. Brethren churches should and do keep these things in mind and practice them for the glory of God and the strengthening of the Body of Christ.

Review Guide

Preface

1. Re-read the Preface for a general overview and focus of the book.

Making God Number One

1. The biblical basis for worshiping may be first understood from Genesis 1 & 2 where a huge hint is given, that the one who created all things deserves our ceasing from regular labor to honor him (Gen. 2:2). A more specifically articulated ground for God's worship is given in the Ten Commandments. What is established in the Preamble of the commandments?

2. What is one of the chief purposes of the Ten Commandments?

3. What is the purpose of the first commandment?

4. The first commandment calls for total commitment to the one true God. Why is this so? What are some of the other gods which people allow to be number one in their lives? How about you?

5. Why did God forbid the Israelites to worship other gods?

Worshiping the One True God

1. How would you define and describe idolatry?

2. What are the differences in focus of the first and second commandments?

3. What are the two prohibitions given in the second commandment?

4. What are some of the reasons why it is wrong to fashion a physical image of God?

5. What is meant by worshiping God in spirit and in truth?

6. What are some conclusions or applications which may be drawn from the second commandment?

Keeping the Lord's Day

1. What is the issue presented in the fourth commandment?

2. Why is the Sabbath a rest and worship day?

3. What else may be permitted on the rest and worship day?

4. What are the stages in the development of the Christian rest and worship day?

Ordering Worship

1. According to John Stott, why is worship the priority task of ministry? What is your view, and why?

2. What are the two overall purposes of corporate worship? What scriptures support them?

3. What are the three characteristics worship planners should keep in mind, as John Stott identified them?

4. What are the dangers or consequences of worshiping without biblical guidance?

5. What skeletal outline for worshiping do we discern in Isaiah 6:1-8?

6. Contrary to general understanding among evangelicals, what do the Millennials prefer in the worship setting? How would you describe the nature of these preferences?

7. What are the shortcomings of giving excessive attention to the "I" and "me" expressions of the faith which are so

Review Guide

prominent in the worship of many churches? What may be neglected?

8. Although the styles of conducting classic and contemporary services of worship may differ, what inclusions are basic and should be present in any service of public worship, and in what order?

9. What are some of the values of thoughtfully-ordered services of worship?

10. What are some of the elements of synagogue worship which were carried over into early Christian services?

11. What are the distinctly Christian elements?

12. Review the Guide which gives the biblical basis for the elements of public worship. In your estimation, which ones are essential, and which may be variable, and why?

Praying in Worship

1. As you review this chapter, keep a running list of some of the reasons why congregational prayers in worship are beneficial. For example, in what way is the order of worship intended to benefit us in our private praying? What are the main areas of inclusion of both the order of worship and our personal prayers?

2. What is the biblical principle for group praying? And what is there about the Lord's Prayer which helps us understand the appropriateness of the congregation praying it together in worship?

3. What passage of scripture helps us appreciate the *collect* form of prayer? What are the five parts of a collect? Using the suggested form, write one of your own which would be suitable as an Invocation to be prayed by the pastor; or one for the congregation to pray as a Prayer of Confession.

4. What are some of the ways the pastor assists the congregation in the prayer elements of worship? What prayers in particular may the pastor pray for the congregation?

5. When might a Pastoral Prayer be suitable in a worshiping assembly, and when is it unnecessary?

Praying the Lord's Prayer

1. What are two reasons why the Lord's Prayer is named appropriately? Explain.

2. In addition to the plurals of the Lord's Prayer, how does the Lukan version support the congregational use of it in worship?

3. What ideas from the writings of William Barclay, Herman Witsius and G. Campbell Morgan with regard to rabbinic practice of prayer help us appreciate the use of the Lord's Prayer in worship?

4. What are the values and potentialities of the Lord's Prayer? Discuss especially the Lord's Prayer as a "compendium of the gospel" and the confessional import of the congregation praying it in worship.

Preaching With a Manuscript

1. What are the various approaches or methods of sermon delivery?

2. According to the author, what are the values suggested for manuscript preaching?

3. In your view, what are its weaknesses and why? What would be needed for effective manuscript preaching?

4. If you are a pastor, will you preserve your sermons; if so, in what ways will you do so for future reference for you and anyone else in your congregation?

Music in Worship

1. What are several significances of music in worship?

2. What three primary functions of vocal music are discussed?

3. What might a church choir, worship team, or other vocal ensemble understand to be their roles in worship? How may that understanding help them in their rehearsing and singing in the worship service?

4. What might instrumentalists understand their roles to be in worship?

Rite of Dedication

1. In what way may we understand the rite of dedication as an acted sign?

2. What are the ceremonial acts the Jews practiced which provide the basis for the Christian rite of dedication of infants and young children?

3. What is involved in administering the rite? How do you or your church practice it? What additional thoughts might you have regarding how it may be practiced? Do you believe the rite important for families and churches? If so, in what ways do you think it is? If you do not think it is necessary, what is your reasoning?

Signing Repentance

1. In some Christian traditions the imposition of ashes is practiced on the first day of the Lenten season. Even if your church has not practiced this, it is worth understanding why some do. Why do they? What is the significance of the observance?

2. What is the biblical understanding of repentance to which the rite of the imposition of ashes is related?

3. What values might you attribute to the custom of Ash Wednesday? If you know little about the historical development of Ash Wednesday or other aspects of the Church Year as observed in many churches, take some time to investigate that in a worship dictionary or on the internet.

Making a Spiritual Commitment

1. List, define and describe the various terms or expressions in the Bible for making a spiritual commitment.

2. What terminology does your church use? Does it convey sufficiently all of the meanings new converts to Christianity should understand?

3. Does your church include within your worship service a time for persons to make a public profession of faith in Christ? Do you believe that is an appropriate time to do so? What other ways may be employed than the ones with which you are familiar?

Rites of Christian Baptism and Confirmation

1. What are the antecedents of our Christian practice of baptism?

2. Why are people baptized today? That is to say, what are the purposes of Christian baptism?

3. What are the varieties of meanings attached to Christian baptism?

4. What is the purpose of the rite of confirmation?

5. What are the values of participating in the actions of immersion baptism?

6. If you are a pastor, how might you administer baptism and confirmation which differs from the description given in the chapter?

Review Guide

Church and Membership

1. Discuss the difference between the church invisible and the church visible. Give scriptures to support each meaning.

2. Describe the significances of conceptualizing the church as the Body of Christ.

3. What should be the criteria for receiving people into local church membership? Is baptism necessary for that? Explain with biblical support why or why not you believe the way you do.

4. How may we understand the responsibilities of being members of local churches?

5. Is official church membership important? Give biblical references for your position.

6. What are your congregation's criteria and public practices for receiving persons into membership?

7. Does your church have a class for perspective members? If not, what ways are offered for the orientation and instruction of persons before they are received formally as members?

8. What Brethren resources do you use in their preparation?

Rite of Holy Communion

1. Discuss the difference between the terms *ordinance, sacrament* and *rite*. Which do you prefer, and why?

2. Have you read any of C. F. Yoder's *God's Means of Grace* or *The Soul of the Symbols* by Joseph Shultz? Ask your pastor how you may acquire or borrow copies to read.

3. How does an understanding of the Jewish Day of Atonement contribute to your appreciation of the significance of the elements of Holy Communion?

4. How may we think of Holy Communion as being evangelistic?

5. How does your church observe the Love Feast? How often? Given the Bible's teaching on the subject, how often do you think the Love Feast should be observed? Does the Bible give evidence for observing the Eucharist alone? If so, how often do you think it may be offered? What might be the values of more frequent observance?

Rite of Feet-washing

1. Do you understand John 13 as obligatory for the rite of feet-washing? Why or why not?

2. What is symbolized and thus instilled in believers' lives when they practice feet-washing?

3. How does your church practice the rite?

Rite of Anointing

1. How may we think of the rite of anointing as a means of God's grace being imparted?

2. What are some biblical references for the basis of the practice?

3. What may be the inclusions practiced and the emphases communicated and instilled in the administration of the rite?

4. How is anointing administered in your church?

The Spiritual Discipline of Fasting

1. How may a *spiritual discipline* be defined?

2. What devotional concept lies at the heart of fasting?

Review Guide

3. Fasting was viewed by the Jews as one of three essential devotional disciplines. What were some of the times or occasions when they fasted?

4. What do we learn about fasting from the accounts of the prophetess Anna and of the ministry of Paul and Barnabas?

Index

acted signs, sign-action, 97, 113-114
adoration, 28-29, 36, 43, 47, 56
anointing, anoints, 98, 100, 119, 138, 155-161
Aquinas, Thomas (c.1225-1274), 59
Arminius, James (1560-1609), 122 (& note)
ascription of praise, 56
Ash Wednesday, 101
ashes, 101-102
Ashton, Joseph N. (1868-1946), 80
atonement, Day of Atonement, 113, 139-143, 166
authoritative orders, 137
Ayo, Nicolas, 59, 64 (& note)
baptism, ix, 97-98
baptizo, 113
baptizands, 119
Barclay, William (1907-1978), 149
Barth, Karl (1886-1968), 82
believers baptism, ix, 97
believing in Christ, believing in Jesus, 107-110
Benediction, 43, 57
Berkhof, Louis (1873-1957), 123
biblical worship, 25-36
birth of the spirit, 112
blended, viii-ix, 36
Body, Body of Christ, 53, 55-56, 71, 92, 94, 124, 131, 168
Book of Common Prayer, 47, 51
born again, born anew, 108-109, 111, 129
Brethren, Brethren practices in worship, ix-xi, 29 (& note), 41, 48, 50 (& note), 60, 87, 92, 97, 108, 117, 119, 138 (& note), 143, 147, 152 (& note), 153, 156, 160-161, 163-164, 168
Brumbaugh, Martin Grove (1862-1930), 50 (& note)
Calvin, John (1509-1564), 14, 59, 77, 84, 123, 134, 142
catechesis, catechetical, catechism, catechumens, 134
characteristics of worship/worship orders, 26-37, 42
choral singing, 87-90

CLASSIC WORSHIP

Christ (defined), 98, 157
Church (defined), 37, 122
church invisible, 123, 127
church visible, 123-135
classic, classical, classics, viii-xi, 73, 85, 94, 138 (& note), 161, 163, 168
Classic Order, 41, 44-45
Closing Prayer, 58
collect, 51-54
commitment, 3-4, 56, 111, 128-130
compendium, compendium of the gospel, 62, 64 (& note), 67
concert of prayer, 50
confess, confessing faith, 64-65, 108, 110-111
confession, 28-29, 36, 47, 56
confirmation, confirming, 113, 117, 119
congregational prayers, 47-54, 59-71
consecration, 97, 137
contemporary, viii-ix, 34-36, 41, 45-46, 94
Contemporary Order, 45-46
converted, 108, 112
Cyprian (200-258), 64
Decalogue, 1
dedication [worship element], 29, 36, 43
Didache, 41 (& note)
digest of doctrine, 64, 67
directory for prayer, 59
discipleship, 117-119, 128
doxa, 85
Durnbaugh, Donald, 29 (note), 50 (note)
Edwards, Jonathan (1703-1758), 77, 121
ekklesía, 37, 122
elements of worship, service elements, 40 (& note), 43-46
Ellens, J. Harold, 65
endowment of the Holy Spirit, 117-118
Eucharist, *eucharistía*, 40-41, 137-138, 144, 152
fasting, xi, 163-168
feet-washing, xi, 98, 138, 144-145, 147-153
Flora, Jerry, 155 (note), 158

Index

Hauerwas, Stanley, 64
Henry, Matthew (1662-1714), 5, 57, 60
hilasterion, 141
historic influences, 39-41, 60
Holsinger, H. R. (1833-1905), 50 (note)
holy, 15-16
Holy Communion, xi, 17-18, 60, 97-98, 130 (note), 137-146
holy kiss, 153
immersed, immersion, ix, 113, 115, 119
imposition of ashes, 101, 138
index prayer, 67-68
initiation, 130, 132
instrumental music, 90-93
intercession, 47, 56-57
Invocation, 53-54, 57, 62
Jehovah, 2
Jeremiah, David, 60
Justin Martyr (c.100-c.165), 40 (& note)
Kimbrough, S. T., 82
Langer, Suzanne (1895-1985), 79
laying on of hands, 98, 117, 138
Lehman, James H., 50 (note)
leitourgía, 37, 48
liturgy, 25, 37, 41
Liturgy of the Upper Room, 40 (note)
Liturgy of the Word, 40 (note)
Lord's Day, 20-21, 155
Love Feast, xi, 60, 97-98, 137-146
Lord's Prayer, 48, 56, 59-71
Lord's Supper, 40, 137-146, 135
Lucado, Max, 60
Luther, Martin (1483-1546), 60, 64, 67, 77, 80, 134, 164
Mack Sr., Alexander (1679-1735), 134, 138
making a spiritual commitment, x, 107-112
mark of identity, 61, 70
membership, xi, 121, 127-135
memorial, 137

metanoeo, 103
Millennials, 31-32
monotheism, 8
Morgan, G. Campbell (1863-1945), 64, 67
Morse, Kenneth I., 29 (note), 50 (note)
music in worship, x, 79-95
nacham, 103
nesteuo, 166
Opening Prayer, 53-54
ordering worship, order(s) of worship, ix-x, 23-47
ordinance(s), x (& note), xi, 134, 137-138
outline for private praying, 47
pardon, words of assurance, 28-29, 36, 43
Pastoral Prayer, 56-57
plurals [of the Lord's Prayer], 61
polarization, 35, 94
polytheism, 8
potentialities [of the Lord's Prayer], 63-71
praise and worship, 94
Prayer of Confession, 43, 53-55
Prayer of Intercession, 43, 55-56, 63
Prayer of Thanksgiving, 40, 43, 55
praying in worship, x, 47-71
praying the Lord's Prayer [in worship], x, 59-71
preaching with a manuscript, x, 73-78
preamble, 1-2
priesthood of believers, 53
principle of agreement, 49
proclamation, 28, 36, 43
profession of faith, 133
public response, 116, 118
purity of intention, 165-166
purposes of worship, 24
rabbinic practices in prayer, 61-62, 68
receiving Christ, receiving Jesus, 108-112
repentance, 101-106
rest and worship day, 16-17, 21

Index

rite(s), *ritus*, ix-xi, 97, 117, 161
Rite of Anointing, xi, 155-161
Rite of Christian Baptism, x, 113-119, 138
Rite of Confirmation, x, 113, 117, 119
Rite of Dedication, x, 97-100
Rite of Feet-washing, xi, 147-153
Rite of Holy Communion, xi, 137-146
royal priesthood, 135
Sabbath, *shabbat*, 15-16, 18-21
sacrament, *sacramentum*, xi, 137
sanctification of time, 15
saved, 108-111
Schaff, Philip (1819-1893), 64, 67
Schilling, S. Paul, 82
Schwarzenau, ix
self-dedication, 113, 118
servant-hood, servant nature, 147, 152 (& note)
service elements, 40 (& note), 43-46
Shultz, Joseph, x (note), 138 (note)
sign-action, sign acts, 97, 113-114
sign union with Christ, 115
significance of music in worship, 80-84
signing repentance, x, 101-106
signing with oil, 117
spiritual commitment, 4, 107-112
spiritual disciplines, xi, 163, 168
Sproul, R. C., 124
stages of [worship] development, 19-21
Stagg, Frank, 60
Stoffer, Dale R., 50 (note)
Stott, John R. W., 23, 62, 68
substitutionary atonement, 140, 142
sum, 166
sumphoneo, 50
system or body of divinity, 59, 63
Ten Commandments, 1-2, 4, 6, 17
Ten Words, 1, 6, 13

Tertullian (c.150-220), 64 (& note), 67
thanksgiving, 47, 137
theological categories, 41, 43-44
three-fold administration [of the Love Feast], xi, 161
three-fold immersion, x
traditional, traditionalists, viii-ix, 35, 60, 94-95
triune immersion, 119, 161
union with Jesus, united with Christ, 108, 112, 116, 118
Upper Room, 98, 137-138, 143-144, 147, 152
values of manuscript preaching, 74-78
values of participation, 118, 138
values of praying the Lord's Prayer, 63-71
values of worship orders, 37-39
vocal music, 85-90
vows, 132
Warren, Rick, 31, 130
Watson, Thomas (1620-1688), 59, 63-64 (& note)
Watts, Isaac (1674-1748), 57, 81
Webber, Robert, 31-32, 38-39
Wesley, Charles (1707-1788), 81
Wesley, John (1703-1791), 77, 82, 123, 165-166
Whitefield, George (1714-1770), 77
Willimon, William, 64
Willoughby, William G., 50 (note)
Winthrop, John (1588-1649), 131
Witsius, Herman (1636-1708), 62-63
work of the people, 48
Yoder, C. F. (1873-1955), 138 (& note), 156 (note)
Yom Kippur, 113, 139
Youssef, Michael, 61

Biography

PETER E. ROUSSAKIS (b. 1946), a native of Connecticut, has served in ministry since 1971. At the time of publication he is Pastor of the First Brethren Church of Burlington, Indiana, affiliated with The Brethren Church, the denomination of his ordination, headquartered in Ashland, Ohio. Concurrently he serves as Director of Sacred Music Studies and the Charles Wesley Professor of Sacred Music for the Graduate Theological Foundation, South Bend, Indiana. Dr. Roussakis has served as a minister of music and Christian education in Kentucky and Ohio, a professor of church music in Texas, and a combination pastor and music minister in New Hampshire. Within the Brethren Conference of Indiana he has served as Moderator, on the Executive Board, and on the Ministry of Pastoral and Congregational Care. He and Phyllis (Berkshire) were married in 1970. They have two sons.

BS, MS, Southern Connecticut State University
MCM, Southern Baptist Theological Seminary
STM, Boston University
DMin, Austin Presbyterian Theological Seminary
PhD, Graduate Theological Foundation

MANCHESTER COLLEGE LIBRARY

3 9315 01045334 5

264.06 R762c
Roussakis, Peter E.
Classic worship

DATE DUE

WITHDRAWN
from
Funderburg Library